PROCLAMATION COMMENTARIES

**The Old Testament
Witnesses for Preaching**

Foster R. McCurley, *Editor*

Genesis, Exodus, Leviticus, Numbers

Foster R. McCurley

FORTRESS PRESS Philadelphia, Pennsylvania

To
Scott, Brett, and Dana
through whom
"God has made laughter for me"
(Genesis 21:6)

Library of Congress Cataloging in Publication Data

McCurley, Foster R
  Genesis, Exodus, Leviticus, Numbers.

  (Proclamation commentaries)
  Bibliography: p.
  Includes index.
  1. Bible. O.T. Genesis—Criticism, interpretation, etc. 2. Bible. O.T. Exodus—Criticism, interpretation, etc. 3. Bible. O.T. Leviticus—Criticism, interpretation, etc. 4. Bible. O.T. Numbers—Criticism, interpretation, etc. I. Title.
  BS1225.2.M32   222'.1'06   78–14670
  ISBN 0–8006–0593–4

7406A79   Printed in the United States of America   1–593

CONTENTS

FOREWORD

This present volume concludes *Proclamation Commentaries–The Old Testament Witnesses for Preaching*. Like its New Testament counterpart, this series is not intended to replace traditional commentaries which analyze books of the Bible pericope by pericope or verse by verse. This six-volume series attempts to provide background material on selected Old Testament books which, among other things, will assist the reader in using *Proclamation: Aids for Interpreting the Lessons of the Church Year*. Material offered in these volumes consists of theological themes from various witnesses or theologians out of Israel's believing community. It is our expectation that this approach—examining characteristic themes and motifs—will enable the modern interpreter to comprehend more clearly and fully a particular pericope which contains or alludes to such a subject. In order to give appropriate emphasis to such issues in the brief form of these volumes, the authors present the results, rather than the detailed arguments, of contemporary scholarship.

On the basis of its concern to address the specific tasks of preaching and teaching the Word of God to audiences today, this commentary series stresses the theological dilemmas which Old Testament Israel faced and to which her witnesses responded. Accordingly, the historical and political details of Israel's life and that of her ancient Near Eastern neighbors are left to other books. Selected for discussion here are those incidents and issues in Israel's history which have a direct relationship to the theological problems and responses in her existence. Since the Word of God is always addressed to specific and concrete situations in the life of people, the motifs and themes in these commentaries are directed to those selected situations which best exemplify a certain witness's theology.

Treated in this volume are the first four books of the Bible, the so-called Tetrateuch. Because these books occupy more than eighteen percent of the entire Old Testament and because they have such importance for Judaism and Christianity alike, each one could have been treated in a separate volume. Yet there is some advantage in dealing with the Tetrateuch as a whole, for the overview of history and themes can be helpful for the contextual interpretation of individual passages.

Moreover, the treatment of the Tetrateuch as a whole rather than of individual books is justified simply because Genesis, Exodus, Leviticus, and Numbers were not written as separate books. Through the Tetrateuch run originally distinct narrative strands which discuss the human story and portions of the history of Israel in different lengths and with different emphases. When these strands or sources were merged and combined with the Book of Deuteronomy, the whole was divided into five scrolls, each labeled by a phrase from the opening sentence. The first was called "in the beginning"; the second "these are the names"; the third "and he called"; the fourth "in the wilderness"; and the fifth "these are the words." When this Pentateuch was translated into Greek in the third century B.C., the scrolls were given names which defined their subject matter. Thus arose the names Genesis, Exodus, Leviticus, Numbers, and Deuteronomy.

The last of these, Deuteronomy, is not treated in this volume, because it does not consist of those narrative strands, as do the previous four books. During the first half of this century it was thought that the sources continued through Joshua, thus forming a Hexateuch of similar material. In 1943, however, Martin Noth changed that prevailing view by demonstrating that the Book of Deuteronomy is related to what follows rather than to what precedes. He argued that the law book found in 621 B.C. by Josiah's men in the Jerusalem temple was expanded by the addition of Deuteronomy 1—3 in order to serve as the introduction to the long historical corpus comprising Joshua, Judges, Samuel, and Kings. Further, Noth showed that the narrative sources known as J, E, and P extend only to the end of the Book of Numbers (with a few verses at the end of Deuteronomy attributed to P). Thus Noth reduced the Hexateuch to a Tetrateuch and expanded the Deuteronomistic hisory to include the books of Deuteronomy and Joshua.

The recognition of the Tetrateuchal sources began in 1753 when the Frenchman Jean Astruc discovered that the two names for the deity in the Book of Genesis was due to two originally separate sources. While little attention was paid to his study, during the century following several scholars expanded his findings by isolating four sources from Genesis through Joshua. On the basis of repetitions and duplicate stories, diversities of style, and characteristic words and phrases, there came to light the sources which were called Yahwistic (J), Elohistic (E)—both on the basis of divine names—Deuteronomic (D), and Priestly (P). The process of combining these documents was described in terms of successive redactors (editors) of the original documents.

Various modifications of this four-source hypothesis were proposed. Beginning in 1912 some scholars argued that there were two strata in the J source. Much of the material in the earlier J¹ level has been identified as a separate source but labeled differently: O. Eissfeldt identifies an L (Lay) source; J. Morgenstern a K (Kenite) source; R. Pfeiffer a source S (Seir). Most reasonable, however, is to follow Noth's limitation of the sources to J, E, and P.

At the same time one must recognize that the sun does not rise and set on source analysis. H. Gunkel's work at the beginning of the century introduced form-criticism into the Old Testament by his classic study *The Legends of Genesis*. This attempt to look behind the written sources to earlier forms of expression opened up the understanding of the first books of the Bible to a dynamic development of traditions over centuries of transmission. While numerous studies on various parts of the traditions were produced following Gunkel's principles, none was more comprehensive than Martin Noth's *A History of Pentateuchal Traditions* which appeared in German in 1948 but in English not until 1972. This classic work, though conjectural at many points, opened up a new approach to the complexities of the traditions in the Tetrateuch. It is based on the assumption that behind the sources lies a substantial amount of historical memory.

Recently source analysis has fallen into some disfavor, in part because of an emphasis on the literary structure of the text as we have it, and in part due to an appreciation of a text's context in a given body of tradition or within the canon as a whole. These welcomed insights serve to set the priorities on the text before us rather than on conjectural conclusions regarding the prehistory of the pieces.

Yet source analysis, in spite of some of its limitations, serves a valuable theological function. Because the witness to God's Word always addressed people in the particular circumstances of their lives, because there is no Word of God in the abstract, the messages of the Yahwist, the Elohist, and the Priest—to the extent they can be isolated for study—were powerful expressions of the Word of the Lord for their day. To understand the situation of their audiences and to comprehend their distinctive messages is to know that God truly left the safe abode of the heavens in order to become entangled in the joyful and heartbreaking affairs of human existence. That the Yahwist wrote his story during the tenth century B.C. in Jerusalem when Israel was in her heyday and that the Priest wrote in the sixth century B.C. to the people of Israel in exile, demonstrates the concreteness and the diversity of God's involvement with his people through his inspired witnesses.

The particular theological and ideological emphases of the individual sources have been the subject of significant publications. In his famous essay "The Form Critical Problem of the Hexateuch" (1938) Gerhard von Rad provided a new understanding of the Yahwist as a theologian who merged originally independent traditions (exodus and Sinai) into a unified history of salvation. While few scholars today agree that it was with the Yahwist in the tenth century B.C. that these traditions came together, and while some (especially Rolf Rendtorff) question the theological role of the Yahwist, nevertheless von Rad's work gave impetus to a necessary appreciation of the theological dimension of the sources. The works cited in the bibliography by Ellis, Cross, McEvenue, Habel, Jenks, Brueggemann, and Wolff are particularly helpful in advancing our understanding of the sources as proclamations to their day. Essays by the last two mentioned scholars have been collected in the volume *The Vitality of Old Testament Traditions,* which stresses the theological problems to which the "kerygma" of each source was addressed.

At the same time the redactors who combined the sources, and the editors along the way who rearranged and added material, also addressed their audiences in particular situations. For example, it seems that if J were a Jerusalem source and E a northern one, the two would not have come together until the fall of Samaria in 721 B.C. There is good reason to suspect that J and E were merged shortly after the fall of the northern kingdom as a means of joining in Jerusalem northern and southern traditions and hopes. Thus a new situation, the fall of the North, gave rise to serious theological questions, and precisely at the points of combining J and E some of the answers to those questions might lie. Likewise the trauma of the destruction of Jerusalem and its temple, as well as life in the land of exile two centuries after the destruction of the North, surely caused some of the old stories to be reinterpreted in a new light.

Thus the Tetrateuch is a dynamic record of God's involvement with his people in the numerous situations of the first two millenia B.C. In its pieces and in its entirety God spoke anew to each generation and in every place his people were located. Traditions were handed on, written down, reinterpreted—all according to the changing needs and experiences of the people. The dynamic impact of the stories and their witness to God's activity and presence led even New Testament writers to interpret and reinterpret their messages, motifs, and imagery in witnessing to the new event which occurred in Christ.

As this series comes to an end with the present volume, I take this opportunity to express appreciation to Fortress Press for the invitation to serve as series editor and for the complete cooperation I have enjoyed, particularly from Norman Hjelm, former director of the press, and from Martha Onusconich, whose help and patience were especially supportive. Finally I express special gratitude to Jannine Baumann, student at the Lutheran Theological Seminary, who served as copy editor for this six-volume series. Her concern for detail and consistency alleviated substantially my editorial work on this project.

Winter, 1979   FOSTER R. MCCURLEY
                          Lutheran Theological Seminary at Philadelphia

CHAPTER ONE

THE ORDER OF THINGS

Statements about creation from a faith perspective attempt to evaluate that which has come into being and to understand its role in the order of things. Whether a person of faith views creation negatively (as in Hinduism) or positively (as in the Bible), the issue at stake is the relationship of the created life both to whatever caused its origin and to other created things.

Among many of ancient Israel's neighbors, creation stories seem to have been determinative not only for the beginning of life but also for its continuation. For example, when the Babylonians recited at New Year's time their creation story, the *Enuma elish,* they not only described an ancient heavenly battle between Marduk, the creator of order, and Tiamat, the monster goddess of chaos. Rather they believed that through their recital and ritual dramatization of the story, creation itself was taking place and ensuring the continuation of life for another year. The role of the gods in the phenomena of nature and the role of humans as the gods' slaves in the world, defined the relationship between the two worlds which was maintained by ritual drama (for the story, see *ANET,* pp. 60–72).

Apart from such determinative approaches to creation common throughout the ancient Near East, there existed another way of viewing relationships in the created world. It was a sober observation of, reflection on, and listing of the phenomena of nature in order to understand the world's order and human participation in that order. An example of this intellectual approach to creation is the Egyptian "Memphite Theology of Creation" (see *ANET,* pp. 4–6). Here, in an attempt to establish the cultic importance of the town Memphis, that city's god Ptah is said to have conceived the elements of the universe and to have brought them into existence by his speech. "Indeed, all the divine order really came into being through what the heart thought and the tongue commanded" (*ANET*, p. 5). At the end of this god's creative activity, we read "And so Ptah was satisfied" (footnote: OR "so Ptah rested").

The Old Testament employs the bizarre battle imagery common among Israel's neighbors (e.g., Ps. 74:13–14; Isa. 51:9–10) and simultaneously reflects on creation more soberly (see Pss. 8, 104), but it is in the two narratives of Genesis 1—2 that creation theology takes its predominant form. These narratives are not isolated stories or reflections, as creation was treated among Israel's neighbors. Rather they are merely the beginning of extended narratives which have as their primary concern the creation and role of Israel in God's world.

While the two creation stories at the beginning of Genesis do not contradict each other, they nevertheless are separate stories addressed to audiences at different times and in different places. The first story comes from the hand of the Priest in the sixth century B.C. (labeled P); the second from the tenth century B.C. theologian called the Yahwist (J). Their distinctiveness can be observed by a simple outline describing the sequence in which the various phenomena were created.

Genesis 1:1—2:4a (P)	*Genesis 2:4b–25 (J)*
lights	male human
firmament	garden
earth, planets, vegetation	vegetation
sun, moon, stars	rivers
birds, fish, beasts, serpents	beasts, birds
humankind (male and female)	female human

In addition to this differing sequence, other significant divergences appear: (1) the state of the universe before God began to create was watery chaos, according to P; for J it was a waterless desert; (2) the title for the deity in P is "God" (Heb. Elohim); for J, "the Lord God" (Heb. Yahweh Elohim); (3) the narrative style of P is formal and repetitious; of J, casual and down-to-earth; (4) the concept of God is likewise formal in P; in J the Lord God is portrayed as a hard-working craftsman but one who does not plan ahead.

Before these two stories were joined by the Priestly redactor, each one made its own particular witness to the Word of God which met certain needs in the life of Israel. Although each story is based on older elements, the forms in which we have the stories now is a particular proclamation concerning God as Creator, and each one deserves its due.

GENESIS 1:1—2:4a

The Priestly account of the creation, as we have it, is a complex document which defies any certain interpretation. Some scholars argue that the proper background for understanding this first chapter of the Bible is the Babylonian *Enuma elish*. Others, for reasons obvious in the previous discussion of Egyptian reflections on creation, point to the Memphite theology as the key to unlock the mysteries.

Whatever the background—if indeed only one can or should be isolated—it seems that the Priestly writer composed his work during the exile in Babylon in the sixth century B.C. He addressed himself to the exiles who had been brought from Jerusalem in 597 and in 587 B.C. and to the many Jews who were born in Babylon. Those exiles knew all too well the grandeur that was Babylon's. They could hardly have missed the New Year Festival when the god Marduk was carried in triumphant procession after his combat with Tiamat. Surely they heard the story of the *Enuma elish* over and over again. They were saturated with the knowledge that Marduk was king of the gods and creator of the universe.

Polemic Against the Sacralization of Nature

In this setting the Priest put together some old traditions and made his witness. His story of creation begins, like the Babylonian one, with a watery chaos. Whether the first verse should be translated "In the beginning God created . . ." (*RSV; KJV*) or "In the beginning of creation, when God made heaven and earth . . ." (*NEB*), is not as important as the view expressed in verse 2 that the condition of the world before God spoke was a chaotic mess of darkness, deep, wind, and water—all unformed substances. The mythological impact of this one verse is overwhelming and probably reflects a variety of backgrounds. "The earth was *tōhû wābōhû*." Gerhard von Rad suggested that *bōhû* is related to a certain Baau, the nocturnal goddess in Phoenician mythology (*Genesis,* p. 48; but cf. his revised edition, p. 50). In Genesis 1:2, however, *bōhû* has no personality or divine status; it is simply part of the chaotic primordial state. Surely, mention of "deep" (*tᵉhōm*; no definite article in the Hebrew) must have called to mind that monster of chaos named Tiamat (actually the same Semitic word, the final *t* being a femine ending in Babylonian). Yet neither "darkness" nor "deep" has personality; they no longer represent a hostile force to the creator God. Thus Genesis 1:2 is loaded with mythological expressions, but they are demythologized to represent nothing more than the uncreated nature of the world. As such, even *tōhû wābōhû* is used elsewhere to describe the condition of a land after Yahweh has brought his judgment upon it (Jer. 4:23; see also Isa. 34:11).

That same concern to depersonalize, desacralize, and demythologize nature recurs in the chapter. (1) The assignment of the waters "into one place" (v. 9) recalls both the confinement of Tiamat by Marduk (*Enuma elish* IV 140; see *ANET,* pp. 66f.) and the apparent enclosure of Yamm by Baal (III AB A; see *ANET,* pp. 130f.). But in Genesis no battle occurs; no monster is vanquished; it is only water—not Deep, not Yamm—which is located in one place. (2) The placement of the heavenly luminaries in the firmament (1:14–19) comes dangerously close to the activity of Marduk after his victory. In *Enuma elish* V the conquering hero established the actual deities in the heavens, assigning to each its proper function (see *ANET,* pp. 67f.). When the Priestly writer describes this portion of the universe, he maintains the divinelike terminology "to rule the day . . . to rule the night . . . to rule over the day and over the night . . ." (vv. 16, 18). The Priest, however, avoids the specific words for "sun" and "moon" which could be understood as deities and uses instead the impersonal "lights" (*mā'ōr*), the word which elsewhere designates the "lamps" in the tabernacle (Exod. 25:6; 27:20; 35:9, 14, 28; 39:37; Lev. 24:2; Num. 4:9, 16). (3) As for the living creatures of the deep (1:20–24), the Priest states explicitly that "God created the great sea monsters." These giants of the deep are not foes to be defeated before creation takes place but rather God's own creatures which he examined and declared "good." Thus the writer of Genesis seems to direct his creation story in polemical fashion against the sacralization of nature in the ancient Near East, particularly against that in Babylon where his audience was living in exile.

Polemic Against the Enslavement of Humanity

Beyond this view of nature, the Priestly author polemicized against the Mesopotamian view of humankind. In the *Enuma elish,* after Marduk had won his victory, he proposed to create "savage-man" to do the work of the gods "that they might be at ease" (*ANET,* p. 68). The human race was formed out of the blood of slain Kingu, Tiamat's general, and was obligated with the service of the gods. Another Mesopotamian text, used as an incantation to aid in childbirth, tells that humankind was formed out of clay, animated with the blood of a slain god, and given "to bear the yoke of the gods" (see *ANET,* pp. 99–100). The creator deity in this case is a goddess appropriately named Mami.

Against this view that humankind is created to serve as slaves to the gods, Genesis 1 portrays man and woman in royal terms. The writer introduces this final work with the words, "Let us make man in our image, after our likeness; and let them have dominion over . . ." the earth and all its creatures (1:26–28). The use of the word "dominion" (*rdh*) alone betrays the high estimation of human-kind by the writer; rather than serve as slaves, humans are to rule. That esteem is confirmed by the fourfold repetition of "the image of God." In light of the connection with "have dominion" the "image of God" seems to have its closest parallel in an ancient Egyptian de-sign in which the deity Amon held the sign of life toward the king and said, "My beloved son, receive my likeness" (Frankfort, *Kingship and the Gods,* p. 161). In Egyptian religion the king in fact became divine on coronation day, but the allusion to the likeness of God in Genesis 1 says nothing about the divinity of the human race, only its dominion. Thus, it seems that the royal image of humankind stands over against the slave image of Mesopotamia.

Proclamation About Humanity

This treatment of humankind in Genesis 1 already demonstrates that the Priestly account of creation is far more than mere polemic. This positive statement about the nature of the human race leads us to consider further what contributions the writer makes to our understanding of humanity and of the world.

(1) To male and female together is given the command to have dominion over the rest of creation. They are equal partners, kings and queens, in this responsibility of stewardship over the earth and its creatures. This understanding of their royal privilege and responsibility throws the word "subdue" into a certain light. A mere word study of the verb *kbs* leads one to conclude that the term has negative connotations such as enslave, oppress, bring into bondage. However, the Priest uses the word nowhere else throughout his material. We must exercise a great deal of caution, therefore, about interpreting the Priest's "subdue" in a purely negative sense, especially since he has already portrayed the human race as kings and queens over creation. A ruler does not devastate the land but nurtures it, seeks its welfare, and enhances its beauty—even while eating from it and using its resources.

(2) Likewise to the male and female together, God said "Be fruitful and multiply . . ." (v. 28). This "command," introduced by "And God blessed them, and God said to them," is much like the statement regarding the fish and the birds (v. 22). Thus, while the imperative is used in both cases, the words are set in the context of blessing rather than command. Like other cases in the Hebrew Bible, the imperative form of the verb is used for something which is beyond one's own power to accomplish (see Gen. 42:16; Deut. 32:50; Isa. 49:9).

Following H. W. Wolff's method of discerning the kerygma of a given biblical author by identifying a set formula which recurs in key passages, Walter Brueggemann argues that the piling up of the verbs "be fruitful . . . multiply . . . fill . . . subdue . . . have dominion" reflect the kerygma of the Priest as he addresses those in the exilic situation of poverty, defeat, and despair by proclaiming God's promise of transformation into their opposites. Brueggemann posits that the formula has its origin in old land-possession traditions dating from the entry into Canaan and thus speaks to a landless (i.e., exiled) people (*Vitality of Old Testament Traditions*). By this understanding the words "be fruitful and multiply" do not command a worldwide population explosion but promise the blessing of survival in the apparently God-forsaken situation of exiles (cf. Jeremiah's letter to the exiles in which he too urges the continuation and multiplication of the people, Jer. 29:6).

Proclamation About Nature

In addition to these powerful contributions the Priest makes about humanity, he waxes eloquent about the created world. (1) On each day (except the second), when God had finished his creative work, he inspected it like a master craftsman who examines his product and says, "It is good" (cf. Isa. 41:7). Six times God stamped his approving "good" on his created things, and at the end of the sixth day, when he looked at everything he had made, he saw it was "very good" (Gen. 1:31). Perhaps nowhere else in the ancient world is such a positive evaluation placed on created matter and earthly life as here. Indeed, the Bible asserts unequivocally the goodness of all that God made and thus stands in sharp contrast to those religions which regard the material world as evil and detrimental to the "spiritual" nature of humans. As Walther Zimmerli puts it, "The whole thrust of the Old Testament proclamation guards against any flight into a beyond which is turned away from the world" (Zimmerli, *Old Testament and the World,* p. 13). Indeed, even the new heavens and the new earth of the eschaton are portrayed in terms affirming the goodness of the world (see Isa. 65:17–25).

(2) Further, the world which God created is orderly. It is not the whims of gods or the capriciousness of a single creator god but rather the orderliness of the creation God made that enables life to continue. When God established vegetation on the earth, he arranged that the plants and the trees have within them the necessary seeds to replenish their own kind (1:11–12). The heavenly luminaries have as their purpose to serve "for signs and for seasons and for days and years" and "to give light upon the earth" (vv. 14–15). He made the creatures of the sea "according to their kinds, and every winged bird according to its kind" (v. 21), "the beasts of the earth according to their kinds and the cattle according to their kinds, and everything that creeps upon the ground according to its kind" (v. 25). This monotonous literary repetition serves to emphasize the consistency and orderliness of God's creation.

We cannot leave the Priest's creation account without some com-

ments on the methods of creative activity and on the days involved. In the first place, God brought the phenomena of creation
into being by means of three verbs: say, make, create. God's fiat
alone is said to have brought into existence light (v. 3), dry land
(v. 9), and vegetation (vv. 11–12). His fiat is followed by the verb
"made" in connection with the firmament (vv. 6–7), the luminaries
(vv. 14–16) and the beasts of the earth (vv. 24–25). And the divine
"let there be" is carried out by God's "creating" the sea creatures
and birds (vv. 20–21) and also the humans (vv. 26–27). That each
of the six days begins "And God said" testifies to the priority of
this concept by the Priestly writer. Whether or not some other action
verb follows, the writer asserts that just as Yahweh's Word effects
deliverance of his people from exile (Isa. 55:10–11) and brings
about historical events of various kinds (the whole Deuteronomistic
history), so his Word effects creation itself.

Much has been made of the fact that eight creative acts are
squeezed into six days. Some scholars have attempted to identify
different sources, and others, various levels of tradition. Little fruit
can be gained from such labor. Though complex in background,
origin, and style, Genesis 1:1—2:4a seems to be a unity, composed
by the Priest on the basis of various traditions at his disposal. It
seems that while the writer felt compelled to deal with eight different
phenomena of nature, he wanted equally to set creation into the
traditional seven-day literary pattern in which an action continues
for six days and "on the seventh day" occurs the climax to that
activity. This pattern, well known from Ugaritic poetry and attested
also in the flood story of the Gilgamesh Epic, is used by the Priestly
writer again at Exodus 24:15–18 where the cloud covered Mt. Sinai
"six days; and on the seventh day he called to Moses out of the
midst of the cloud." The Priest's use of the common pattern in
Genesis 1:1—2:4a serves to extol the "rest" of God, his Sabbath, as
the climax to the creative action. Such an emphasis on the Sabbath is
quite understandable for the Priest speaking to people in exile when
indeed the Sabbath had become especially important as a day of
praise to God.

GENESIS 2:4b–25

The Yahwist's account is more like a paradise story than a creation
story, partly because it is so local. It begins with a description of a

dry desert as the state of things before the Lord God went to work. The Creator formed a man out of dust from the ground and enlivened him by breathing air into his nostrils. Now God needed to find a place for him, and so he "planted a garden in Eden, in the east." In this garden God made to grow all sorts of vegetation beautiful to look at and delicious to eat. Two trees are singled out: the tree of life and the tree of the knowledge of good and evil.

The Lord God then transported the man from wherever he was to the garden "to till it and keep it" (2:15), telling the man that he may eat of any tree in the oasis except "the tree of the knowledge of good and evil . . ., for in the day that you eat of it you shall die." Then, concerned about the sociality of the man, God made the beasts of the field and the birds of the air. But even after man's naming them all, it was clear to God that someone else was needed. And so out of the man's rib, the Lord God created woman. When the man awoke and saw the lovely new creature, he broke into song (v. 23).

Among the many important issues in the story, four are selected for comment here: (a) the nature of the humans and their relationship, (b) the goodness of work, (c) the naming of the animals, (d) the two trees.

Humans and Their Relationship

The human being created by God is strikingly similar to those of Mesopotamian mythology: he is made out of clay (cf. the story of Mami mentioned above; also see the Epic of Gilgamesh, I, where the goddess Aruru "pinched off clay" and made Enkidu [*ANET,* pp. 41–42]). Unlike the humans created in the *Enuma elish* and by Mami, however, the force that brings life to the clay figure is not the blood of a god. Nor is this $n^e\check{s}\bar{a}m\hat{a}$ that God breathes into the man some phantomlike soul. It is a "breath" of air. Thus immediately the man is defined not on the basis of a divinity's blood but on the basis of God's action of blowing air. There is nothing here to suggest the immortality of the man—not even of something *in* the man. There is only clay and air and utter dependence on the Lord God for life.

God's concern for the man is evident not only in the provision of food but in the sexual companionship of a woman. The Yahwist has been accused of being the Bible's first male chauvinist, not only because the male was created first but also because the woman fulfilled the role of "a helper fit for him" (vv. 18–22). Neither of these issues leads to the superiority of the male over the female. In the first place, that the woman was created last could lead to the conclusion that she is the pinnacle of creation, just as the last created in Genesis 1 are the man and the woman. Second, the translation "a helper fit for him" *(RSV)* is not as accurate as it could be. Better is "a help as his counterpart," for the Hebrew $k^e neg d\bar{o}$ must mean something like "as the one opposite him, counter to him." But this rendering still has in it the word "help," implying that the woman is to be man's assistant. Such a distortion can be discounted immediately when one realizes that the word "help" (*'ēzer*) is used elsewhere in the Old Testament only in reference to God. "Help" comes from the Lord (Pss. 20:2; 121:1–2; 124:8), and indeed the Lord himself *is* "help" (Exod. 18:4; Deut. 33:7; Pss. 33:20; 70:5; 115:9,10,11; 146:5). Thus, far from denoting an inferior position, the word "help" assigns to the woman a term used only for God himself. While this terminology in no way leads to a divine status for the woman, it does render unacceptable any view which considers the woman to be inferior. Indeed, it is for this woman that the man leaves his father and mother and cleaves to his wife (v. 24).

The two counterparts stood before each other in all the physical splendor with which God endowed them "and were not ashamed" (2:25). This is the order of the sexual relationship as God created it: male and female who correspond to each other in such a way that they help and love each other beyond every other human relationship —a striking assertion in the midst of a society where planned marriages were the order of the day.

Such a story about the unabashedly sexual relationship among humans is equally as striking in the Yahwist's environs. In the Canaanite fertility religion it is Baal's sexual activity that was emphasized. When Baal was incapacitated by Mot (Death), the soil was infertile, animals were impotent, and humans were disinterested. But when sister Anath demolished Mot to free Baal, the fertility god wasted no time in rejuvenating his waned prowess. Either with Anath herself or with a cow (the text is too fragmentary here) Baal became the father of a wild ox/buffalo, and apparently all nature joined in— even religious worshipers with cultic prostitutes (for Baal's revival see *ANET,* pp. 140–142).

Against all that, the Yahwist tells his creation story about a God who is virtually asexual. The Lord God participates in no sexual act in order to make the trees grow in the garden or to excite the passions of the humans. And rightly so! The Lord has no female counterpart —here or anywhere else in the Old Testament. Although God is called "Father," the term is used in an adoptive or relational sense (see e.g., 2 Sam. 7:14; Jer. 31:9). He no more participates as a male in the conception of his children than physically he suffers the travail of a woman at birth, even if he seems to have a womb (cf. Job 38:29; also see Deut. 32:18). The title "Father" as well as the labor of childbirth are equally metaphorical images to express God's relationship with his children.

A god who is asexual needs no cultic prostitution in worship. Therefore, the sexual activity between the man and the woman in Genesis 2, and throughout the Bible has no cultic significance. Their attraction to each other does not serve some religious need but is a result of the relationship which God gave for their mutual pleasure and commitment.

Likewise, the Priestly writer of Genesis 1 makes no mention of God's sexual activity. God's word "Let us make man in our image" addresses not a female partner but his heavenly court (see Isa. 6:1–8; 1 Kings 22:19–33; Job 1). For the Priest, male and female reflect the image of God, and that image in them takes the form of heterosexual relationships which result in the blessing of progeny. Thus, for J and P alike, and for the entire Bible, sexuality is exclusively a human characteristic which is a blessed gift from an asexual God.

The Goodness of Work

In a sense Eden does not qualify as a paradise because the man is set in the garden to work: "to till it and keep it" (v. 15). It seems at first glance that the "slave of the gods" view common in Mesopotamia is present here as well. What is different here, however, is the fact that the garden is not—as in many mythologies—the garden of the gods but a garden made solely as a place for the man to live. Thus the work that man was to carry out is not for God's benefit but for his own.

Work is part of God's intended order in creation. It occurs in the garden *before* the Fall and so is not to be attributed to sin. Work is good in this story, just as work will be good in the eschatological day when God creates a new heavens and a new earth (see Isa. 65:21–23). It is good because it is not done in vain; one benefits from the labor of the hands.

Naming the Animals

When God made the animals of the field and birds of the air, he brought them to the man "to see what he would call them; and whatever the man called every living creature, that was its name" (v. 19). What lies behind this piece of the story is the ancient Semitic idea that a person or thing did not merely have a name (although this is clearly part of the story); a person or thing and their names were intimately related to each other. Knowing another's name meant intimate knowledge of the other and even the possibility of control over the other. With this understanding it is possible to interpret Genesis 2:19 in such a way that man was given control over the animals. Thus the writer of Genesis 2 asserts the same supremacy of humans over the other creatures that the Priest makes so explicitly by his verb "have dominion."

Another feature of this naming-the-animals caper is the intellectual pursuit of man in discovering, defining, and ordering the world around him. In much the same manner as the wise men who collected information about virtually everything and developed thereby a "list science" for the purpose of understanding and participating in order (cf. 1 Kings 4:33), the first man exercised his rational powers in naming the animals. It is in this close relationship and on the basis of their names given by humans that the animals are given their rightful place in the world's order (see also Isa. 11:6–9; 65:25).

The Two Trees

The tree of the knowledge of good and evil and the tree of life appear together at the beginning of the story (v. 9) and at the end (3:22). It is sometimes argued that these trees represent originally separate stories and that the Yahwist has woven them together to deal with the first humans and their defection in one sweep (see Westermann, *Creation,* pp. 72–76). The trees themselves play an important role in the story. While in the Old Testament the tree of life is nothing more than a figure of speech (see Prov. 11:30, 13:12; cf. Ps. 1:3), in this story the tree of life represents the food of immortality which always is denied to humans. The hero Gilgamesh lost his plant of life to a serpent (*ANET,* p. 96) and by a clever divine scheme Adapa rejected the banquet of life-giving food (*ANET,* p. 102).

As for the tree of the knowledge of good and evil, its function in the story is to place a limit on human freedom. God is Creator, and the humans are his creatures; the lines of authority are not to be confused. With that function in mind a likely interpretation of the knowledge of good and evil is the freedom to experience everything. The Hebrew word "know" (*yāda'*) involves much more than intellectual awareness; it includes the realm of intimate experience (cf. Gen. 4:1 and Amos 3:2). As for the good and evil, it seems that the two opposing parts are intended to convey the whole of experience.

Thus the nature of the humans as God made them includes the freedom to enjoy every plant and tree in the garden—with an exception! The freedom is limited by God's prohibition which separates the humans from the gods. God is God, and the creature is creature. Any failure on humans' part to keep the lines clearly drawn will surely lead to death.

These are the faith statements about creation which the Yahwist and the Priest have given us. Their positive evaluation of the material world is startlingly refreshing. Yet their primary interest seems to lie in the basic relationships which God established "in the beginning": Creator to creation, Creator to human creatures in particular, humans to the rest of creation, and male to female. The New Testament had another relationship to add: Christ. While early Christians seem to have assumed what the Old Testament proclaimed about God and creation, their witness in creeds and hymns affirmed Christ's relationship to God as the firstborn of all creation and his relationship to all things which exist in and through him (1 Cor. 8:6; Col. 1:15–20). We shall see in the following chapters that because of their interest in these relationships, neither the Yahwist nor the Priest were concerned about creation per se. Rather they wrote their stories of Genesis 1 and 2 in order to lead to the relationship of Israel to God and his created world.

CHAPTER TWO

A MATTER OF LIFE AND DEATH

After his creation story the Yahwist proceeds immediately to the motif of rebellion by the humans—first in the garden, then east of Eden where fratricide reveals the extent of the disharmony. J continues with several genealogies, a brief story about the divine-human marriages, the long flood narrative, more genealogies, and finally the Tower of Babel story. It seems that in this general framework for this history of humankind in Genesis 2—11, the Yahwist followed an existing pattern known from the Mesopotamian Atrahasis Epic where the sequence of creation-rebellion-flood is attested (see Lambert and Millard, *Atrahasis: The Babylonian Story*).

Whatever the background for the Yahwist's human history, the importance of his story lies in the use to which he put his material. The story in Genesis 3—11 tells of the actions of humans and of the Lord's response to their actions. Incorporated into that story are several genealogies in which positive cultural achievements were made by humans: building cities (4:17; 10:8–14), raising cattle (4:20), developing music (4:21), forging metal (4:22), and planting vineyards (9:20). However, in the dramatic narratives about humans which the Yahwist recorded, the actions of humanity are viewed negatively as self-glorification, even self-deification, and so the Lord responded consistently with punishment in the form of expulsion. The tenth-century theologian of Jerusalem collected, edited, and arranged these stories in order to portray a universal history of rebellion which will serve as the motive for the Lord's intervention into a particular history, that which begins with Abraham in Genesis 12:1–3.

THE FIRST REBELLION

The road to death begins with the enticement of the woman by the serpent. The woman was able to hold her own on the issue of the forbidden fruit until the serpent retorted "You will not die. For God knows that when you eat of it your eyes will be opened, and you will be like God [or gods], knowing good and evil" (3:4–5). With that possibility in mind, the woman streaked down to the midst of the garden, took the forbidden fruit, and ate it. It was good to look at, delicious to eat, and able to make wise—a total experience. Along came her husband, and instead of childing her, he too joined in the picnic. All of a sudden, they felt shame and guilt and nakedness, and so they covered their private parts with fig leaves.

The nature of their deed was clearly disobedience brought about by a desire to "be like God." They had stepped over the limits of their freedom by their desire to experience all things without restriction, authority, or limitation. The man and the woman together attempted to break down the barrier between Creator and creature and thus to play God. It happens to all humans who constantly devise the rules to suit selfish desires rather than to live as the creatures God made. The story of Adam and Eve is not a unique experience; it is the story of every human being. "All have sinned and fall short of the glory of God" (Rom. 3:23; cf. also 5:12).

The result of their deed was, first of all, shame at their nakedness. Before their rebellious act, the man and the woman rejoiced in each other's naked splendor; now they could no longer appear before each other without guilt, embarrassment, and shame. And so their disobedience against God resulted first in the rupture of their relationship with each other.

The results, however, did not end there. When the Lord God took an evening stroll in the garden, the trembling couple—at first in hiding—admitted what they had done but typically passed the buck about who was really responsible. The man said it was the fault of the woman "whom thou gavest to be with me" (3:12). The woman said it was the serpent who beguiled her. Ignoring all the excuses, God meted out the bad news.

The serpent was cursed beyond all other animals; he was to crawl on his belly and eat dust. The hostility between the serpent and the woman would extend to generations following. The reference to "her seed" followed by "he shall bruise"—so *RSV*—is not a prophecy about Christ or Mary, as Luther believed, but rather points in a collective sense to future descendants, humans in general. (See the translation of the verse in *NEB, TEV,* and *The Torah.*)

Just why it was the serpent out of all the animal kingdom who was singled out by the storyteller as the tempter is difficult to say. Perhaps it was a polemic against the veneration of the serpent as a symbol of healing in the ancient world (cf. the use of the bronze serpent as a snakebite cure at Num. 21:4–9). Perhaps the notion of the serpent as the symbol of chaos in the creation conflict stories serves the writer here to explain why the order of God's intended relationships has gone askew. Or maybe the creature appears here because in the Gilgamesh Epic from ancient Mesopotamia, a serpent was the villain who ate the hero's plant of life, thus depriving Gilgamesh of immortality, as Adam and Eve were deprived in this story.

The woman was not cursed, but the judgment on her fell into two areas: (1) childbearing will be painful, and (2) her husband will rule over her. That which was to be the beautiful experience of bringing into the world a new life in the form of a baby, now—as a result of her rebellion—will be marred by pain in delivery. The equal partnership with the man, her counterpart, now has been changed into a subservient role with her husband as ruler. From here develops the concept of the woman as the man's property to be disposed of at his will (Deut. 24:1–4). Such subordination is due, then, not to God's created order but to human sin. The proper relationship can be restored only by the gospel of Jesus Christ (see Gal. 3:28).

Likewise the man was not cursed, but because of him, the ground was cursed. The fertile soil from which the man himself was made (2:7) and with which a relationship was basic to life was no longer a source of blessing, but a curse. As a result, his tilling and keeping of the ground which was such a positive task in 2:15 now becomes a matter of toil. Previously work was good because man would reap the benefits of his labor; now the work is drudgery, the ground full of thorns and thistles. As the various forms of the Hebrew word for "toil" ('ṣb) show, the drudgery is as much emotional and attitudinal as it is physical. Presumably, muscular stress was part of the tilling and keeping to begin with; now the work has become the proverbial "pain in the neck." Finally, man's original relationship with the ground can be restored only when he returns in death to the dust from which he was taken (3:19).

The man and the woman did not die, as God had threatened. Apparently the serpent was right after all: God was not true to his word "in the day you eat of it you shall die" (2:17). Or was he? Immediately after God had finished his pronouncements and after Adam had put into effect his new authority by naming Eve, God expelled them from the garden before they could eat also of the tree of life (3:22–23). From this description it must be concluded that the humans were created as mortals; they could have grasped immortality, but they had not yet eaten of the food which gives eternal life. Like Gilgamesh and Adapa, the first human pair in the Bible did not take advantage of the possibility of immortality when it was in their hands.

If humans were mortal from the beginning, why did they not die on that day? In a sense they did. God cast them out of the garden, and so they no longer lived in the close relationship of Eden with him and with each other. The *shalom*-like life of Genesis 2 lasted only until "the afternoon of the first day," as Luther put it. Now it was not wholeness and completeness of life (the root meaning of *shalom*) but fragmentation, discord, and strain that characterized human existence. Previously the humans were mortal; now they were dead besides.

God was indeed true to his word. But before he expelled them from Eden, the Lord himself made for the first couple loincloths of skin and clothed them. Even in the midst of his judgment, God demonstrated his care for the creatures he made, rebellious though they were. Then the Lord sent them out to live and work "east of Eden." John Steinbeck's novel of that title makes clear what such life is like: destroyed marriage, conflict between father and son, brother and brother. In fact, in the Bible it leads to fratricide. Cain, the first born, kills Abel, and the parents are no longer part of the story.

The story in Genesis 4:1–6 is told not to extol one occupation over the other, but to relate one more account of rebellion and its consequent expulsion from the ground and from the presence of the Lord. The storyteller does not explain why the Lord accepted the animal offering of Abel but not the fruit offering of Cain. But as a result of the discrepancy Cain was filled with anger. In a fury that began at a sacrificial altar of God, Cain killed his own brother in the field, spilled his blood on the ground, and thus took upon himself the prerogative of God over life and death.

Just as the Lord appeared immediately after the disobedience of Adam and Eve, so too God confronted Cain directly after his attempt to "be like God." In the garden episode the Lord called out, "Where are you?" Here God asked, "Where is your brother?" But Cain's response was even worse than that of his parents: he lied directly to the Lord's face and denied any responsibility for his brother's welfare. Like the degeneration of father to son in Mario Puzo's *The Godfather* where son Michael killed his brother-in-law and even his own brother, and lied about the former to his wife, so here the generation east of Eden is even more hardened than the parents.

And so too is the judgment of God. After Adam's rebellion the cursed ground would yield food only through the worker's toil and sweat. Now the ground, cursed by the blood of the slain brother, will yield no food at all. Cain, once the tiller of the ground, was now expelled—like his parents; he became a fugitive and a wanderer in the earth to be fair game for any would-be slayer.

Yet the Lord placed on Cain a mark—not of disdain (as in our contemporary metaphor) but of protection, like the one placed on the foreheads of the people who decried the abominations in Jerusalem (Ezek. 9:4–6). Thus in the midst of severe judgment—expulsion from the ground and from the near presence of the Lord—Cain knew that God had the last word: it was a word of grace in spite of human horror.

CHAOS REVISITED

The sixth chapter of the Book of Genesis opens with a peculiar story. The sons of God—gods—took a fancy to human women and married them. The Lord's response seems at first to be inappropriate to the act: "My spirit shall not abide in man forever, for he is flesh, but his days shall be a hundred and twenty years" (6:3). The sons of God married, and the Lord talked about mortality! The text proceeds to mention that the Nephilim were on the earth in those days, then seems to return to the marriage problem to speak of the resulting offspring who were warriors renowned from of old.

God's response to the divine-human marriages is not so strange when one realizes that behind the scenes is the age-old problem of failing to keep clean the lines between the gods and the humans. Whether the story reflects a notion that in sexual intercourse, properties of one partner are conveyed to the other, or a belief that through the marriages divine-human offspring would be born (so perhaps v. 4), the issue at stake is the one separating the heavenly beings from the earthly ones: immortality. That the Lord set down the limit of one hundred twenty years demonstrates his continued insistence that the two realms be kept apart. Once again, God drew the line at immortality, just as he did in Genesis 3.

While the origin of the story is obscure, it seems safe to conclude that the episode was not composed in order to introduce the flood story. However, in its present position in the Bible and its place in the Yahwist's narrative, the story now functions, along with God's regrets about making humans (vv. 5–8), as a powerful motive for the Lord's decision to send the flood.

The flood story continues from this point through 9:17. Unlike the creation stories in which J and P are set side by side, the two stories here are interwoven in intricate fashion. The Priestly editor seems to have kept most of the Yahwist's work, and so two rather complete sources can be separated as follows: J is preserved at 6:1–8; 7:1–5, 7–10, 12, 16c, 17b, 22–23; 8:2b–3a, 6–12, 13c, 20–22; P is apparent at 6:9–22; 7:6, 11, 13–16b, 17a, 18–21, 24; 8:1–2a, 3b–5, 13ab, 14–19; 9:1–17. Thus there are two flood stories in the Bible which have been combined skillfully into one.

Flood stories from Mesopotamia are striking by comparison and by contrast to Genesis 6—9. In ancient Sumerian literature from the early second millenium B.C., there appears a flood story in which the gods decreed destruction of humankind by a flood. A human king named Ziusudra was warned in a dream by the god Enki and instructed to build a ship. A storm raged for seven days, at the end of which Ziusudra offered sacrifices to the sun god. Thereupon, the gods granted immortality to Ziusudra who became "like a god" (cf. Gen. 3:5).

The Babylonian Gilgamesh Epic, also from the first half of the second millenium B.C., contains a flood story. Gilgamesh, the semi-divine king of Erech, was distressed by the death of his friend and battle companion Enkidu. The necessity of facing his own mortality led the hero to seek his distant ancestor Uta-napishtim, the sole survivor of the flood. In the eleventh tablet of the epic Uta-napishtim ("he found life") told Gilgamesh this story of the flood. When the gods decreed that a flood should devastate humankind, the god Ea warned Uta-napishtim in a dream about the coming disaster and instructed him to build a ship. The vessel, a cube seven stories high, was to serve as the lifeboat for the man and his family, as well as for all kinds of animals. Heavy rain and storm battered the land for six days, at the end of which the ship came to a halt on the top of Mt. Nisir. The hero sent out a dove, a swallow, and a raven to see if dry land were available in the distance. Finally, on Mt. Nisir, Uta-napishtim offered sacrifices which "smelled sweet" to the gods. Thereafter immortality was bestowed on Uta-napishtim and his wife, and the goddess Ishtar made herself a necklace as a sign of remembrance.

As the story continues, Uta-napishtim taught Gilgamesh that while the gods reserved immortality for themselves and made of him and his wife the only human exceptions, one could remain eternally young by eating of a certain plant of life, to be found only by a difficult and arduous trek. Gilgamesh accepted the challenge, found the plant, and headed homeward with his magical herb. On the way a snake ate his plant of life. Thus there remained only the survivors of the flood as the exceptions to the gods' rules on immortality.

Particularly striking as a parallel to the biblical flood story is the Atrahasis Epic in which is related the creation of humans by the gods in order that the blood-animated clay beings might serve as slaves. But a population explosion among the humans led to more noise than the gods, particularly Enlil, could stand for a good night's sleep. And so the gods agreed in council to control the problem by plague, then by drought. In each case, the human king Atrahasis entreated his personal god Enki to find ways to avert disaster. Finally, because the human noise continued, Enlil decided to flood the earth. Enki warned Atrahasis in a dream, then elaborated more fully the impending disaster and laid out plans for a ship. The boat was built and loaded with the hero's possessions, with animals and birds. As the flood wiped out the rest of humankind, the gods began to regret their decision—since they had eliminated their work force. At any rate, when the ship of Atrahasis came to rest, the hero offered sacrifices to the gods. Then the mother-goddess Mami made for herself a lapis lazuli fly necklace as a reminder of her lost off-spring.

The biblical story of the Flood is strikingly reminiscent of those other stories in many details: the warning of the hero by a god; the building of a ship; the cargo of hero, family, and animals; the resting place on a mountain; the sending out of raven and dove; the sacrifice of the surviving hero which smells sweet to the god(s); a sign of remembrance/covenant. Interestingly it is not one source or the other but the combination of J and P which provides continuing parallels with the other stories.

The Priestly redactor interwove the originally separate stories in such a way that there is no needless repetition of details in which they might virtually have been identical. Only in J is the instruction to enter the ark maintained (7:1); only in J is reported the sending out of the birds (8:6–12). However, only in P do we read that Noah was warned by God and instructed to build an ark (6:13–16) and that the ark came to rest on the mountains of Ararat (8:4).

There are, however, some different emphases in each of the two sources which the final redactor chose not to harmonize but to maintain in tension. According to the J source, Noah was instructed to take on board seven pairs of clean animals, and one pair of unclean (7:2–3). P, however, tells of God's instruction to take a male-female pair of all animals into the ark (6:19–20; 7:13–16a). Thus it is not the Priest but the Yahwist who is concerned about the ritual distinction of clean and unclean animals. In the same way, it is the Yahwist and not the Priest who records the offering of sacrifice by Noah and the favorable response by God (8:20–21). While one might expect the Priest to be concerned with such ritual or cultic matters, that writer's sense of consistency prevented him from including such elements in his account: the ritual regulations concerning clean-unclean animals and types of sacrifices were given to Moses at Mt. Sinai. Before that event the Priestly writer avoids such practices and distinctions.

Another tension maintained in the two sources concerns the result of the flood story. According to J, the Lord promised not to curse the ground again (8:21–22). If one recalls the curse pronounced to Adam in Genesis 3:17 ("cursed is the ground because of you") and the effect of Cain's bloodshed (4:11), then the promise to Noah following the flood takes on special meaning. Human sinfulness will not affect the ground or the cycle of seasons; rather on the basis of the Lord's faithfulness, nature will maintain its intended form and sequence. The Priest, on the other hand, leads his story to conclude that God made an everlasting covenant with Noah in which God obligated only himself with the oath that he would not again destroy the earth by flood. The sign of this covenant promise is the rainbow in the sky (Gen. 9:1–17; cf. Ishtar's necklace as a sign of remembrance in the Gilgamesh Epic).

In merging the two accounts into one story, the Priestly redactor produced for us a literary masterpiece in which, as Bernhard Anderson puts it, the first part (6:9—7:24) represents "a movement toward chaos" while the second (8:1—9:17) provides "a movement toward the new creation" (*JBL* 97 [1978] 23–39). The flood story culminates in God's monologue in which he reminds the humans of their creation "in his own image" (9:6), repeats the blessing of fruitfulness promised at creation (9:7), and finally commits himself in covenant that the earth will not again come so close to chaos (9:8–17). Just as God remembered Noah tossing about in the ark (8:1), so he will remember his covenant with all creatures when he sees the rainbow in the clouds (9:12–17).

As for Noah himself, one would surely expect on the basis of the fate of Ziusudra and Uta-napishtim, heroes of their flood stories, that our hero too would be granted immortality at the story's conclusion. Instead, the Yahwist tells the story of Noah's nakedness and the resulting curse on Canaan but blessing on Shem and Japheth. And the Priest wraps up the Noah story by enumerating the days of Noah at "nine hundred and fifty years; and he died" (9:29).

There are no exceptions to human mortality in the Bible. Not even the traditional survivor of the flood received special compensation. "My spirit shall not abide in man forever" (6:3, J) is supported by the Priest—before the flood (5:5, 8, 11, 14, 17, 20, 27, 31), after the flood (11:32), and to the hero of the flood himself, by the stereotypical formula "and he died." God's distinction of himself from his creatures in the issue of immortality is maintained consistently.

All these flood stories raise the question about the historicity of a universal flood. The archaeological evidence shows only that the Tigris-Euphrates Valley was subject to severe local river floods, and in the midst of such a disaster the people quite naturally conceived of the impact in universal terms. More recently, the claims for the historicity of the biblical flood have centered around the discovery of wooden structures on Mt. Ararat itself. When the wood retrieved from the mountain was subjected to radiocarbon testing, however, the results proved that the remains claimed to be those of the ark date from approximately the seventh century A.D. (see the recent book by Bailey, *Where is Noah's Ark?,* and his article in *Biblical Archeologist* 40 [1977] 137–146). Thus there is no convincing evidence to support the claims that the biblical flood story is a historical account of a universal deluge.

The important issue is the use the biblical writers made of the common story. We have already seen that the Yahwist used the story in his outline of the primordial history to demonstrate anew how seriously the Lord takes sinfulness of humankind and the defined limits of creatureliness. The Priest incorporated the old Yahwistic story into his own in order to demonstrate that God brought such judgment on the earth for human violence and corruption that the earth was on the brink of its precreation state of chaos. God nevertheless remembered Noah and his cargo and so transformed once again chaos into order, promising in a covenant oath that never again would he flood the earth to destroy it. At the same time, by pulling the older epic into his own, the Priestly editor was able to enhance the immortality issue of the Yahwist with the stereotypical "and he died" in reference to the flood survivor Noah.

LOST IN TRANSLATION

The final act of rebellion in the Yahwist's prehistory is the building of the city with a tower in the land of Shinar (Gen. 11:1–9). The story tells that originally the whole earth had one language, but that harmonious situation changed when people who had migrated from the east and settled in Shinar decided to build a city and a tower in order to make a name for themselves and prevent dispersal. When the Lord saw what they were doing, he confused their language and scattered them throughout the earth.

The story thus contains two major ingredients: (1) the change from one language to many, and (2) the motivation for that change as the Lord's judgment on the people for their construction work.

1. The explanation of the change from one universal language to many different languages—with which the story begins and ends (vv. 1, 9)—certainly has an aetiological thrust. Surely ancient peoples must have wondered why others whom they met at watering holes spoke different languages. Indeed, an ancient Sumerian story tells that "once upon a time" humankind spoke one and the same language, but the god Enki, the lord of wisdom, "changed the speech in their mouths, brought contention into it, into the speech of man that (until then) had been one" (see Kramer, *JAOS* 88 [1968] 108–111). Likewise the biblical story at Genesis 11:1–9 offers an explanation about the origin of human languages. The story, however, is much more significant than an aetiological tale; it is a description of the relationship between God and humanity.

2. The motivation for the change from one language to many lies in the Lord's decision to put a stop to their activity. The people proposed to build a city (which turns out to be Babylon, v. 9) and a tower with its top in the heavens (v. 4). Their plan was thus to build a ziggurat, a Babylonian temple-tower which in its pyramidal shape allowed the people, or at least the priests, to ascend its many steps to the heavenly penthouse level where the gods lived. The ziggurat was thus a mythical "navel of the earth," an umbilical cord which connected the heavenly and earthly worlds in such a way that the worshipers—at their initiative—could meet the gods. The Etemenanki, the tower of Babylon, indeed served this very purpose, and the name Babylon itself (Bab-ili) means "the gate of god(s)."

The people's plan to build the city and temple-tower was accompanied by their wish to "make a name for ourselves." This desire seems to represent not only human conceit but another attempt to appropriate to the creature what belongs to the Creator alone (cf. 12:2 where the Lord promised to Abraham, "I will make your name great"). Their expressed motive for their building and self-esteem was to prevent dispersion over the whole earth. And so they proceeded with their plans.

Ironically, though the people thought that the tower reached into the heavens, the Lord "came down" to see what they had built.

Apparently what he saw in their work was equal in significance to the first couple's eating of the forbidden fruit. Speaking to his heavenly court as he did also at 3:22, the Lord once more proposed preventative measures. Because "nothing that they propose to do will be impossible for them," he scattered them all over the earth—precisely what the people tried to prevent (v. 4).

Throughout Genesis 3—11 God put down his proverbial foot again and again—but with at least one toe raised in order to prevent complete disaster. In the Eden story, the human pair was driven out and forbidden reentry, but the Lord cared for Adam and Eve by making them clothing. Cain suffered expulsion from the land to become a wanderer, but on the fugitive the Lord set his protective mark. In the Noah story the earth's population, except for Noah and kin, was drowned, but God began creation anew with Noah as the father of many nations. Here in the Tower of Babel story, when even the new generation overstepped the limits of God's intended arrangement, the Lord both scattered them and confused their language. Not only was the divine-human relationship impaired, but human beings had trouble communicating with one another.

At the end of the Tower story, it seems that judgment is the last word—in contrast to the previous judgments. In the midst of their confusion the people were not provided with translators or with a Berlitz school. However, the Yahwist's story moves immediately to the call of Abraham. And the Priest makes the same connection with a genealogy listing the generations from Noah's son Shem to Abraham. With the patriarch begins the promise of God (Gen. 12:1–3) which comes to ultimate fulfillment in the Christ event (Gal. 3:8) and which leads to that day on which the people from many nations—each one in his own language—heard the Galilean disciples tell "the mighty works of God" (Acts 2:1–11). Once again, God has the last word! Pentecost is thus God's final answer to the Tower of Babel.

CHAPTER THREE

THE PROMISES TO ABRAHAM

The traditions of the Lord's dealing with the patriarchs begin abruptly at Genesis 12:1 with the command to Abraham to leave his country and his family. At first the command appears to be a continuation of the story of expulsion from land, as we observed it in Genesis 3—11. But here preceded no account of rebellion by Abraham, no example of playing God—only a harmless genealogy and a note about the movement of Abraham's family from Ur of the Chaldeans to Haran where they settled. Abraham had done nothing rebellious—or anything righteous, for that matter! And so, without any motive regarding Abraham's behavior, the Lord commanded the dweller of Haran to give up his land and family relationships and to go. Moreover, the Lord will show him where to go, will direct him to a new land. Thus begins a new story—a story about God promising land and directing the recipients of that promise to receive it as his gift—a story which continues into the Book of Joshua when the land is distributed to the tribes of Israel.

The new story which begins in Genesis 12 picks up from Genesis 1—2 the primary actor as God. From here on through the Bible the subject is God reaching out to humanity rather than the former story of humanity's vain attempts to become like God. The new story, with God as subject, reverses the consequences of the former condition: from expulsion to invitation, from threat to promise, from curse to blessing. The reversal occurs with God's revelation of himself to individuals: the patriarchs Abraham, Isaac, and Jacob.

THE CALL AND THE PROMISES

The beginning of the Abraham cycle at Genesis 12:1–3 sets the stage for all that follows. After the command to go (v. 1), God set forth unconditionally a series of promises:

I will make you a great nation,
  and I will bless you,
  and I will make great your name
  so that you might be a blessing.
And I will bless those who bless you,
  and him who treats you with contempt I will curse;
and in you all the families of the land shall consider
  themselves blessed (12:3; author's translation).

Five times appears the divine "I will. . . ." The Lord promised (1) that he will make out of Abraham a great nation (*gôy gādôl*) (2) that he will bless him, and (3) that he will make Abraham's name great in contrast to the vain human attempt to accomplish that objective for themselves (cf. 11:4). Without mentioning specifically the promise of a son at this point, the Yahwist's formulations here assume that Abraham and his wife will experience the pitter-patter of little feet. The text, therefore, points forward to "the blessed event" as the beginning of the great nation which eventually God brings out of slavery from Egypt and forms into his own "holy nation" (*gôy qādôš*) at Mt. Sinai (Exod. 19:6). The third promise, that of the great name, points toward the Yahwist's own day, when in the Davidic-Solomonic Empire of the tenth century B.C., God promised to David that he would make his name great (see 2 Sam. 7:9).

Thus these first three promises explain to Israel at the height of her glory—the reigns of David and Solomon—that she has become a great nation not of her own doing but solely on the basis of the promises which the Lord gave to Abraham and faithfully fulfilled. It is significant in regard to this purpose that the promises are unconditional; they are not dependent for their fulfillment on Abraham/Israel or her ancestors. The actor is exclusively the Lord, and the recipient is Abraham/Israel. But the movement of the first three promises carries the reader immediately to the purpose for all this generosity: "*so that* you might be a blessing."

The fourth and fifth promises seem at first glance to represent two sides of the coin: the Lord will bless those who bless Abraham but curse those who hold him in contempt. Yet, as the text is given to us, blessing will be experienced by "those," a plural participle but cursed by "him," a singular participle. According to Hans Walter Wolff, the Yahwist has reinterpreted a cultic formula which appears in its original form at Genesis 27:29b and at Numbers 24:9b (both texts using plurals for both blessing and curse) in order to emphasize the gracious blessing rather than the exceptional curse (*Vitality of Old Testament Traditions,* pp. 52–53).

That understanding is confirmed by the conclusion to verse 3: "in you shall all the families of the land consider themselves blessed." Wolff considers this formula to be the central kerygma of the Yahwist. The tenth-century B.C. theologian addressed his glorious Israel not only with the message that it was Yahweh's faithfulness to his promises that effected their greatness, but with the further proclamation that the foreigners living in her midst are the ultimate objects of Yahweh's concern. The question set before Israel is whether or not the Philistines, Moabites, Ammonites, Arameans, Edomites, Amalekites, and Canaanites (see 2 Sam. 8) have experienced through her the blessing from God. Such blessing might be attained through Israel's intercession (see Gen. 18:16–33, esp. v. 18), through covenant making (Gen. 26:26–31; 31:51–52), through the wisdom of Israel (Gen. 39:5; 41:49, 57; 50:20), and even through worship (Exod. 10:31–32).

The formulas at 12:1–3 begin the history of promise which stretches through the Tetrateuch to his final story, that of Balaam at Numbers 22—24, and 25:1–5 (see Wolff). The first response to the promises is recorded briefly and without comment: Abraham went, as the Lord had told him. Arriving in the land where the Canaanites lived, Abraham visited the sacred site at Shechem, the oak of Moreh (the mythological "navel of the earth," Judg. 9:37). There the Lord appeared to Abraham and offered still one more promise: "To your descendants I will give this land" (Gen. 12:7). And so, with this promise of land, (attached as a secondary interest, according to Wolff against von Rad), the Yahwist begins to work out his scheme through the patriarchs to Moses and beyond to the point of Israel's entering the land.

As the Yahwist continues his account he relates a story told elsewhere (Gen. 20 and 26) about the patriarch passing off his wife as his sister in order to save his own life. The Yahwist's use of the story at 12:10–20 seems to support his theological concern in two ways: (1) Abraham's lie throws into grave danger the patriarchess Sarah through whom the Lord would begin the line of descendants promised in 12:2; (2) the effect of Abraham on foreigners is devastatingly clear when his own lack of integrity brings curse rather than blessing on Pharaoh and his house (12:17). Thus the very first story about Abraham following the Lord's many promises demonstrates that the Lord alone must effect what is promised not only through Abraham but in spite of him. When the recipient of the promise takes matters into his own hands, everything is endangered, and so the Lord himself must intervene.

THE COVENANT

In Genesis 15 are related two originally separate stories which when pulled together emphasize the twofold promise of descendants and land. The first account at verses 1–6 concentrates on progeny. While the passage is often regarded as the beginning of the Elohist narrative, it might have been an ancient cultic piece which was originally separate from any source. The imagery points emphatically to the promise of an heir and might be related to royal motifs (see Clements, *Abraham and David*, pp. 15–22).

The introductory words "Fear not" (15:1) are used elsewhere in the Old Testament in connection with the Lord's war against his enemies; Israel should have no fear because Yahweh himself will fight for her (Num. 21:34; Deut. 3:2; 7:18; and often). Such battle imagery is enhanced by the use of Yahweh's self-designated metaphor "shield"; the same epithet is used in cultic laments and thanksgivings to confess confidence and hope in the God who will deliver or has delivered the worshiper from enemy assault (Pss. 3:3; 7:10; 18:2, 30, 35; 28:7; 33:20; 59:11; 144:2). On the other hand, "shield" as divine metaphor occurs also in a more general sense. It is used as a means of describing the Lord as one who shows favor to the upright (Pss. 84:11; 119:114; Prov. 2:7). But perhaps more significant for our passage is the use of the "shield" metaphor as the basis for the blessing of progeny (Ps. 115:9–15) and as the source of confidence that "every word of God proves true" (Prov. 30:5).

Following the self-identification formula appears the announcement "your reward shall be very great" (*RSV*). Other translations emphasize the action of God by following the reading of the Samaritan Pentateuch: "I will make your reward very great" (*NAB*), or "I am giving you a very great reward" (*NEB*). In either case, with "reward" as subject or object, the term seems at first glance to contradict the Yahwist's claim in 12:1–3, 7. The term "reward" seems to imply that Abraham has done something to deserve what follows. While the term *śākār* appears often as the wages which one earns (e.g., Num. 18:31; Deut. 15:18; 24:15; Ezek. 29:18, 19, etc.), the word has other meanings as well: security (Zech. 8:10), hope (Eccles. 9:5), deliverance from exile (Isa. 40:10; Jer. 31:16), and most significant, the inheritance of sons (parallel to *naḥªlâ* at Ps. 127:3). Thus a translation such as "your heritage shall be very great" would be true to the meaning of the word *śākār* and at the same time completely consistent with God's promises to Abraham elsewhere.

Not incidentally, then, the passage begins with God's assurance to "fear not" and with his self-identification as a "shield" whose word is effective. The text continues to offer once again the promise of the Lord that he will make for Abraham a great heritage. Abraham's response in this context is completely understandable: "I continue childless." It seems to Abraham that a certain Eliezer, either a son born to Abraham through one of his servants or an adopted child who would care for an aging father (see the Sale-Adoption text from Nuzi, *ANET,* p. 219), will inherit the estate. Thus Abraham had made his own arrangements in light of the Lord's procrastination. But Yahweh's response to the patriarch's plan is plain enough: "This man shall not be your heir; rather one who comes forth from your own organs will be your heir" (v. 4). Then the Lord led him outside and showed him the dark sky; as many as the stars would Abraham's descendants be. Abraham trusted the Lord's promise, and "he reckoned it to him as righteousness." While Paul uses this verse as an example of justification through faith rather than through works (Gal. 4:3), the emphasis in Genesis 15 is on God's recognition that Abraham appropriated the divine plan to himself.

The extensive use of cultic language in Genesis 15:1–6 indicates that the piece is cultically formulated and perhaps not an original part of the Yahwist's story. The frequent use of terms and formulas attested only in the Psalter is unusual for J. But whatever its origin, this passage about the Lord's promise of descendants serves the same purposes that the Yahwist delineated in 12:1–20: in spite of the clear promises and assurance of God, Abraham makes his own attempts to secure himself; nevertheless the Lord continues in his own way to fulfill his blessing. This time the confidence of Abraham in the Lord's promise of descendants lasted only until the next chapter where the Yahwist records that since Sarah was still barren, the woman gave to Abraham her Egyptian maid Hagar in order to produce offspring (16:1–14). Thus was born the boy Ishmael.

The second account in Genesis 15 concentrates on the gift of land. Verses 7–22 describe a covenant-making ceremony in which the Lord assured Abraham of his promise to give him land. Again, as in verse 1 the Lord introduced himself, this time by the name Yahweh and with the explanation that it was he who brought Abraham "from Ur of the Chaldeans, to give you this land to possess" (v. 7). When Abraham asked for some assurance that he would indeed possess the land, the Lord instructed him to make two rows of dissected animals—and to set down whole a turtledove and a young pigeon. After driving away the birds of prey who descended for a feast, Abraham felt "a deep sleep" and in parallel fashion "a dread and great darkness" fell upon him. Then after an inserted speech about the exodus from Egypt (vv. 13–16), the action continues: "When the sun had gone down and it was dark, behold a furnace of smoke and a torch of fire passed between these pieces. On that day the Lord cut a covenant with Abraham, saying, "To your descendants I will give this land . . ." (vv. 17–21).

Our only means of interpreting the significance of this strange rite is the parallel in the Book of Jeremiah. Here the Lord announced judgment on the people of Jerusalem for their failure to set free their Hebrew slaves during the sabbath year. The bad news is proclaimed:

> And the men who transgressed my covenant and did not keep the terms of the covenant which they made before me, I will make like the calf which they cut in two and passed between its parts . . . their dead bodies shall be food for the birds of the air and the beasts of the earth (Jer. 34:18–20).

Thus, the ones who pass through the parts of the dissected animal in this covenant ceremony commit themselves to the fate of the animal if they are not faithful to the terms promised.

In Genesis 15:17–18 it is none other than Yahweh who passes between the rows and thus who takes upon himself the unconditional obligation to give the land. The "furnace" and "fire" are the symbols of the presence of the Lord in Jerusalem (Isa. 31:9); the "torches" and the "smoke" are some of the signs of the Lord's theophany at Mt. Sinai (Exod. 20:18). Thus the response to Abraham's "How do I know . . ." (v. 8) is Yahweh's commitment of himself to extinction if he is not faithful to his promise.

In spite of the appearance of "Ur of the Chaldeans"—a phrase which came into use only at the end of the seventh century B.C.— most scholars have regarded this covenant rite as "of great antiquity" (Alt, "God of the Fathers," *Essays*, pp. 84–85). Some have connected it with the "god of the fathers" cult (so Alt), while more recently it has been interpreted as a local cult legend of Mamre between the god El and Abraham (so Clements, *Abraham and David*). In either case, it is generally believed to have been incorporated by the Yahwist in Jerusalem during the Davidic Empire as a means of continuing his explanation of how Israel became a great nation and took possession of the land of Canaan.

It is worthy of note that the expression "to possess it" with regard to land occurs nowhere else in the Yahwistic source, but the exact expression *lᵉrištāh* appears twenty-five times in Deuteronomy, twice in Joshua (1:11; 13:1), and once in Ezra (9:11). Of the twenty-five occurrences in Deuteronomy, ten passages combine the verb "give" (Heb. *nātan*) with "to possess it" (*lᵉrištāh*)—as in Genesis 15:7. Moreover, while parallels for covenant making are cited often from the ancient Near East (especially Mari), there is no precise parallel to the ritual here except for the late seventh-century B.C. text of Jeremiah 34. Finally, even the expression "cut a covenant" (*kārat bᵉrît*) of Genesis 15:18 is not used for the theological covenant involving God/Yahweh in any undebated J text. The sources of Exodus 23:32; 24:8; 34:10, 12, 15, 27 are highly questionable. The expression *kārat bᵉrît*, however, is employed for the theological covenant between Yahweh and Israel at Deuteronomy 4:23; 5:2, 3; 9:9; 29:1, 25 and more than thirty times in the following Deuteronomistic history.

It seems possible, then, that the story of Genesis 15:7–22 had been redacted rather severely sometime toward the end of the seventh century B.C. or more likely in the exilic period of the sixth century B.C. If the latter possibility has merit, then the story would address the exiles of Babylon with the message that Yahweh guaranteed unconditionally the land and so he would return them—just as he promised for the slaves in Egypt in verses 13–16. While it might seem strange for someone of the Deuteronomic/Deuteronomistic school to proclaim such assurance on the basis of a theophany (see Deut. 4:12–16), we should recall that "a deep sleep fell on Abraham" (cf. 1 Sam. 26:12), and so he saw nothing at all.

Whatever the origin of the Lord's covenant with Abraham, the story would have suited the purposes of the Yahwist in the tenth century B.C. and would also have been a dynamic expression of Yahweh's unconditional guarantee of land to exiles of a later time. Such is the power of the Word of the Lord as it encounters each situation anew.

Apart from brief interludes here and there, the Priestly writer of the sixth century B.C. contributes only two stories to the patriarchal tradition: Genesis 17 and 23. The first of these stories is the Priest's parallel to the call of and covenant with Abraham and the promise of a son. But far more than a duplication, Genesis 17 portrays the covenant with Abraham as eternally valid for Israel, and thus nullifies the need for another.

After a brief record of the birth of Ishmael (16:15–16), the Priest reports that the Lord appeared to Abraham with an introduction, an invitation, and a promise.

I am El Shaddai.

> Live before me that you might be perfect,
> and I will set my covenant between me and you,
> and I will cause you to multiply exceedingly (17:1–2).

Then the Priest explicates these promises of "God Almighty." Abraham will become "the father of a multitude of nations" (vv. 4, 5); he will be made "exceedingly fruitful" (v. 6), and the covenant given here to Abraham will extend through generations of descendants as "an everlasting covenant" (v. 7) in which El Shaddai will be God for the patriarch and his seed. Immediately there follows the promise of land, "the land of your sojournings, all the land of Canaan, for an everlasting possession" (v. 8). Earlier God made an "everlasting covenant" with Noah and every living creature on earth, the content of which was no more destruction of the earth by flood (Gen. 9:8–17). Now God gives an "everlasting covenant" with Abraham and his seed, the content of which was relationship with himself and the gift of the land of Canaan.

How tightly the Priest ties together his major narratives! After the Flood he repeated twice the blessing to be fruitful, multiply, and fill the earth (9:1, 7) as Noah was to begin anew the history of humanity to whom the manifold blessing was given at creation (1:28). Now in the covenant with Abraham, God promised to multiply him exceedingly (17:2) and make him exceedingly fruitful (17:6). God's plans for blessing now take the form of the creation of a people. For the Priest neither the creation of the world nor the creation of Israel can be separated from each other.

Just as the Yahwist portrayed the covenant with Abraham as the unconditional gift of Yahweh, so here the Priest emphasizes exclusively the action of El Shaddai with one divine "I will" after another. Even the directive to Abraham, "You shall keep my covenant . . ." (17:9) is followed by the act of circumcision as "a sign of the covenant" (v. 11). Failure of an individual to identify oneself by this sign shall be regarded as covenant breaking (v. 14); but the covenant between God and Abraham and his descendant Israel is eternal. Circumcision, then, for Israel—at least in the time of exile—was a confessional act by which an individual appropriated to himself the gift of the eternal relationship between God and Israel.

The promise of land remains unfulfilled in the Tetrateuch for the Priest as for the Yahwist. But the exilic theologian adds a touch of class when in Genesis 23 he relates that after Sarah died, Abraham bought from Ephron the Hittite the cave of Machpelah which was east of Mamre, that is, Hebron (23:19). In this surprisingly dramatic story, comparable to Neo-Babylonion "dialogue documents," (so Tucker, *JBL* 85 [1966] 77–84) Abraham acquired a "possession for burial" in which Sarah and later the patriarch himself were laid to rest on their own turf.

But the immediate concern in Genesis 17 is to begin the growth of the family tree by the promise to Abraham that Sarah will bear her own son (vv. 16–17). The equality with which God speaks of the woman is striking: as Abraham is to become the father of a multitude of nations (vv. 4, 5), so Sarah shall be "a mother of nations; kings of peoples shall come from her" (v. 16). One can hardly avoid recalling the Priest's understanding of the simultaneous creation of male and female "in the image of God" (1:27).

Abraham's response to the announcement is one of uncontrolled laughter. Surely God lost track of the years: Abraham is now ninety-nine years old, and his wife only ten years younger (v. 17). Pulling himself together, Abraham proposed—typically—a plan of his own. "O that Ishmael might live in thy sight" (v. 18). God would have none of it (cf. 15:4). Sarah will give birth to a son; with him God will establish a covenant as an everlasting relationship for his descendants. As for Ishmael, child of Abraham, God would bless him with the creation blessing of fruitfulness and make him a father of twelve princes and a great nation. But the covenant is reserved for the son to be born "at this season next year" (v. 21). A laughing matter, of course! And so he is to be named Isaac ("he laughs").

Now the point of the Priest's birthday calendar becomes clear: he recorded that Abraham was seventy-five years old when he left Haran (12:4b), eighty-eight years old when Ishmael was born (16:16), and an even one hundred when Isaac would wail his first cry (17:17). With Sarah only ten years behind, it was becoming more and more incredulous—even impossible for human biological reasons—for the couple to have a child. And that's precisely when God worked the miracle—to show that the fulfillment of God's promises is exclusively his own doing, that not even human cooperation is to be credited with any share of the outcome.

In the following chapter the Yahwist makes the same point. After hosting three visitors, among whom was the Lord, Abraham received the news that Sarah would have a son the following spring. The narrator tells us that "it had ceased to be with Sarah after the manner of women" (18:11). This time it was Sarah who laughed as she eavesdropped on the conversation. Now the Lord himself put the crux of the matter squarely before Abraham: "Is anything too wonderful for Yahweh?" (v. 13). Then he repeated his promise that he would return and that Sarah would have a son.

THE GIFT AND THE TEST

Finally the blessed event arrived. At Genesis 21:1-7 all three sources J, E, and P join in the birth announcement. Verse 1a seems to be J; verses 1b-5, P; verse 6, E; and verse 7, J. It is all so brief. The event for which Abraham and Sarah had waited for twenty-five years (according to the Priest's reckoning) and for which we, the readers, have been pacing the floor for nine chapters is described with astonishing brevity. We hear nothing more than that he is born and weaned (v. 8). But what is important for the meaning of the stories is explicit enough: "The Lord visited Sarah as he said, . . . as he promised . . . at the time of which God had spoken. . . . God has made laughter for me."

> Every word of God proves true;
> he is a shield to those who take refuge in him (Prov. 30:5).

The Lord is faithful to his promises, and so the way to peoplehood has begun. The child of promise is here!

But he is apparently short-lived. Before we are told of the joys that the aged father experienced with his new son, the writers confront us with a shocking story. The first record of the relationship between Abraham and Isaac begins thus:

> After these things God tested Abraham, and said to him, "Abraham." And he said, "Here am I." He said, "Take your son, your only son Isaac, whom you love, and go to the land of Moriah, and offer him there as a burnt offering upon one of the mountains of which I shall tell you" (22:1-2).

God asked that the long-awaited son be given up as a sacrifice, and Abraham set out to follow the command with unswerving faith. As father and son journeyed up the mountain to the designated spot, Isaac pointed out that they had forgotten the lamb for the burnt offering. In a response in which Abraham seems to point to the resolution of this tragic scene, the father says, "God will provide (*yir'eh*) himself the lamb for a burnt offering, my son" (v. 8). Abraham prepared the wood, bound up Isaac, laid him on the sacrificial altar, and took the knife to slay his son. Just then, an angel of the Lord called from heaven to stop the deed, because "now I know that you fear God" (v. 12). As Abraham looked up, he saw a ram caught in a thicket. As a substitute for his son, the animal was sacrificed, and so the place was named "The Lord will provide" (*Yahweh yir'eh,* v. 14).

The powerful story seems to have undergone a long history of development. The charactertistics of the Elohistic source are clear in the present story: (1) the name Elohim ("God" in vv. 1, 3, 8, 9, 12), (2) the test of people by God (see E's concern at Exod. 20:20) which leads up to the recognition that Abraham fears God (v. 12; cf. 20:11; 42:18; Exod. 1:17, 21; 18:21; 20:20—all E), (3) the communication through an angel (v. 11—a necessary means of communication for the Elohist's transcendent God). When these characteristics of E are stripped away, there is left a story which relates the will of God that an animal be substituted for a child in sacrifice. Whether this old story describes a rite connected with a particular sanctuary called *YHWH yir'eh* (so Noth, *History of Pentateuchal Traditions,* pp. 114f.) or whether it was simply a narrative form of the legal prescription of Exodus 13:11–16, it seems that the Elohist had before him a story regarding child sacrifice.

The Elohist reinterpreted the story as a matter of testing faith— as is clear from his introduction to the story (v. 1). The patriarch passed the test by showing that he "fears God." Hans Walter Wolff has shown that this phrase is the kerygmatic thrust of the Elohist: speaking to his situation in the northern kingdom of Israel during the ninth-eighth centuries B.C., the Elohist asserted that God tests his people through hard trials in order to lead them to "fear God" (*Vitality of Old Testament Traditions,* pp. 67–82). In this particular story, Abraham demonstrates that when God demands obedience, the one who fears God does not hold back what is most precious.

But the development of the story is not limited to the Elohist's redaction of an old story. The account lives on with powerful meaning for generations. In the first place, tradition has connected the story to the site of the Jerusalem temple, for in the late text at 2 Chronicles 3:1 Mt. Moriah is the name of the hill that formerly had been called Zion.

Second, the story in Genesis 22 has been expanded in verses 15–18—another speech of the angel to Abraham. What is striking about this second speech is that it seems to contradict what we have seen thus far in regard to the promise from the Lord. Here—in contrast to everything else—the promise of blessing and multiplication of descendants who possess the land is dependent upon the faithfulness of Abraham. Along with this theological change is an array of terms and phrases which are not characteristic of any of our three Tetrateuchal sources. To take a few examples, although the oath formula with which the speech begins appears elsewhere in prophetic preaching, it occurs nowhere else in the Tetrateuch. The formula "like the sand which is upon the seashore" has exact parallels only in the sixth-century b.c. Deuteronomistic history (1 Sam. 13:5; 1 Kings 4:29) and virtually identical parallels only in the same body of literature (Josh. 11:4; Judg. 7:12; 1 Kings 4:20; 2 Sam. 17:11); even "for" (*kî ya'an 'ašer*) in verse 16 is similar only to expressions in Kings, Jeremiah, and Ezekiel; and the even less common *'ēqeb 'ašer* ("because" in v. 18) is exactly the same as 2 Samuel 12:6 and similar to Deuteronomy 7:12; 8:20. The formula "by your descendants shall all the nations of the earth bless themselves" is identical to the Yahwist's Hebrew formula at Genesis 12:3 only as regards the word "all." Every other Hebrew word is different.

Thus, it is by no means unlikely that the story was expanded in the sixth century b.c. to address Israel, the son of God on the brink of tragedy. It came to exiles with the assurance that because of Abraham's faithfulness, the promise of blessing, descendants, and land will be fulfilled—and that the blessing for all nations of the earth will indeed be secured.

Finally, the story seems to live on in the New Testament. In the transfiguration account at Mark 9:2–9, God announces to the three disciples who accompanied Jesus up the mountain, "This is my beloved son" (Greek *houtos estin ho huios mou ho agapētos*). The formula seems to recall, on the one hand, Psalm 2:7, thus confirming Peter's confession that Jesus is the Messiah, the Davidic king (Mark 8:29). On the other hand, the only occurrences in the entire Septuagint of the combination *huios agapētos* ("beloved son") appear in Genesis 22 at verses 2, 12, 16. It seems, therefore, that the announcement to Peter, James, and John confirms also Jesus' statement about himself that he is the son of man who must suffer (Mark 8:31ff.). Like Isaac, Jesus is the son of God's promise who will be sacrificed and then delivered.

CHAPTER FOUR

THE CONTINUING PROMISES AND THE PROMISER

The promises which the Lord God lavished upon Abraham were to be fulfilled in his descendants, and so it is not surprising that many of the same promises were repeated to Isaac and then to Jacob. These two men were as different as night and day: Isaac appears to be a wallflower in contrast to the flamboyant Jacob. Yet God continued his way of promise toward the accomplishment of his purposes through both of them and even in spite of them.

THE PROMISES TO ISAAC (25:19—26:33)

Apart from the mention of Isaac's weaning (21:8) and the story about the testing of his father's faith with the lad as near victim, we learn nothing about the childhood or youth of Isaac. As was the custom, it was his father Abraham who sent out servants to find a wife for the son, and so most of Genesis 24 tells about Abraham's quest and the introduction of the blushing bride Rebekah. Not until 24:62–67 do we, along with Rebekah, meet forty-year old Isaac, and then only in a brief reference to his taking the woman to become his wife.

Like her mother-in-law Sarah, Rebekah was barren—but only for one verse (25:21). In the same one verse the writer tells us that Isaac prayed to the Lord, the Lord granted his prayer, and Rebekah conceived. There is no drama here about the endless waiting of the barren woman; no continuous record of the patriarch's attempts to solve the problem of childlessness on his own; there is only lip service paid to the barrenness even though twenty years passed (25:20, 26) before the problem was resolved. Rebekah conceived and gave birth—to twins!

The brevity of the entire episode leads the reader to believe immediately that the traditions about Isaac will not be as colorful or suspenseful as those about Abraham. This new patriarch does not seem to have had about him the magnetism which draws legendary material to himself. And that first impression is confirmed when we discover there is only one chapter which preserves the Isaac traditions: Genesis 26—a story which seems to stand apart as an intrusion into the continuing saga between the last verses in chapter 25 and the first verses in 27.

Because of a famine in the land, Isaac moved to Gerar where he met Abimelech, "king of the Philistines" (26:1). In this place the Lord instructed the patriarch not to go down to Egypt, as was usual in the case of famine (12:10; 42:1; 43:1) but to stay put as a sojourner. As the speech continues, the Lord repeated the promise of blessing, of a multitude of descendants, and of land (vv. 3–4). The divine address concludes

> and by your descendants all the nations of the earth shall bless themselves: because Abraham obeyed my voice and kept my charge, my commandments, my statutes, and my laws (vv. 4b–5).

As in Genesis 22:15–18, the terms and ideas here seem to indicate exilic composition, or at least redaction. To give some examples, the pledge of Yahweh to "fulfill the oath which I swore" (v. 3) has its only exact parallel at Jeremiah 11:5, but the similar "keep the oath which I swore to your fathers" occurs over forty times in Deuteronomy; the "nations formula," as in 22:18, has nothing in common with the Yahwist's formula in 12:3; "because . . . obeyed my voice" is a formula common in the Deuteronomistic history (cf. especially Deut. 7:12; 8:20; 2 Sam. 12:6), and the list "charge, commandments, statutes, and laws" occurs elsewhere no earlier than Deuteronomy and is common in that book and in the books of Kings (e.g., Deut. 6:2; 8:11; 11:1; 1 Kings 2:3; 9:6; 11:11; 2 Kings 17:13; 23:3).

The function of the speech is the same as the repeated reference to the Lord's keeping the oath to the fathers in the Book of Deuteronomy: to stress the faithfulness of the Lord in fulfilling the promises he made in the past. That message, permeating the whole Deuteronomistic history, addresses exiles with assurance that God's word is effective (see the same emphasis in other exilic theologians at Genesis 1 and Isaiah 55:10–11).

The Yahwist's own narrative which begins in verse 1 continues at verse 6 with the story that the patriarch Isaac, a chip off the old block, told the folks in the land of his sojourning that his wife was only his sister (cf. 12:10–20; 20:1–18). This repeated trick, regarded by Martin Noth as originally told about Isaac as a warning against the covetousness of Canaanite city dwellers (*History of Israel*, p. 143), serves two functions in the Yahwist's story: (1) it demonstrates that Isaac, like his father, endangered the promise of God by his lie (although the actual danger to Rebekah in this story is minimized) and thus the fulfillment of the promise is entirely the work of the Lord; (2) it explains the origin of the relationship between Isaac and Abimelech, the king who later in the chapter approached the patriarch with the plea that they make a covenant between them. In this covenant making with a Philistine king, the Yahwist demonstrates one more way in which Israel can be a source of blessing for "all the families of the land" (12:3).

THE PROMISES TO JACOB (27—36)

The stories about Jacob are diverse in their geographical settings, in their character portrayals, and in their forms. Essentially, however, they can be classified under three somewhat unrelated headings: (1) Jacob and Esau, (2) Jacob and Laban, (3) theophanies. What unites all three into a meaningful story is the continued faithfulness of the Lord as he works toward the fulfillment of the promises not only through but in spite of the patriarch.

(1) *Jacob and Esau.* The rivalry between the twin brothers seems to begin at the very moment of their birth. The first baby to appear was called Esau because he was red and hairy (not a valid explanation); the second was named Jacob (*ya'ªqōb*) because he had grabbed Esau's heel (*'āqēb*). We are told next of the occupations of the brothers—Esau a hunter and Jacob a tent dweller—and of the love of the father for Esau but of the mother for Jacob. Thus we have the perfect setting for fraternal rivalry (25:27–28).

The first evidence of explicit rivalry occurs immediately (25:29–34). Esau came in from a hard day's work in the field hungry enough to eat a banquet. But all that was available was some lentil soup Jacob was boiling. Esau was welcome to it—at a cost! "First sell me your birthright" (*bᵉkōrâ*). After taking an oath, the starving

Esau sold his birthright and, interestingly, is accused by the story-teller of despising it.

After the interlude of Isaac and Abimelech (26:1–33), the rivalry continues with the note that Esau married two Hittite women, and altogether "they made life bitter for Isaac and Rebekah (26:34–35)—perhaps a justification for the clever scheme of Rebekah which follows. Mother instructed her son Jacob to fetch two kids from the flock for cooking and to dress himself to feel and smell like brother Esau. In this way Jacob could appear before the aging and virtually blind father to receive the blessing reserved for the favorite—usually the oldest—son (27:1–17). The plot succeeded without a hitch, and Jacob received the blessing of fertile land and of authority (vv. 18–29). Then Esau came home and learned of the deception, but it was too late! The word spoken effects what it says: "I have blessed him—yes, and he shall be blessed" (v. 33). The deceived and angered brother cried out, "Is he not rightly named Jacob? For he has supplanted (*'āqab*) me these two times" (v. 36).

Thus with Jacob's reputation as "cheater," it seemed best to his mother that he go away to stay with Uncle Laban in Haran until the heat blew off (vv. 41–45). This is the Yahwist's attempt to relate the traditions of Jacob and Esau with those of Jacob and Laban. The Priest tells his own story about the transition at 27:46—28:9 where Isaac called Jacob to him, blessed the younger son, and charged him to avoid these Hittite/Canaanite girls by finding a wife in Paddan-aram where Laban lived. Upon hearing this charge to Jacob, Esau decided to add to his own collection an Ishmaelite wife who would be more pleasing to his father.

The Priest does not allow an opportunity to slip by. In the midst of the charge to find an acceptable wife, he has Isaac speak that kerygmatic formula we have seen from Genesis 1:28 through the Noah story and down to the covenant with Abraham at chapter 17.

> God Almighty bless you and make you fruitful and multiply you, that you may become a company of peoples. May he give the blessing of Abraham to you and to your descendants with you, that you may take possession of the land of your sojourning which God gave to Abraham (28:3–4).

It seems that the Priest is addressing his audience of exiles in the sixth century B.C. with the message that God will indeed bless the people with fruitfulness in the foreign land and that it is unnecessary—even contrary to his will—to realize that blessing by taking wives from among the foreigners.

Jacob departed and stayed in Haran for some time. The Jacob-Esau cycle resumes at 32:3–21 and 33:1–17 when Jacob made preparations to return home and to encounter his brother Esau who was living now in the country of Edom (see the later identification of Esau as Edom at 25:30 and 36:8). As it turns out, most of the clever plots were unnecessary, because Esau welcomed back his brother with open arms. Jacob then promised to follow Esau at a slower pace to return with him to Seir. In fact, however, Jacob and his caravan bought some land in Shechem and later moved to Bethel—without, it seems, the slightest intention of going to Seir. But the relationship between the two brothers—once one of bitter rivalry—was restored to mutual respect.

(2) *Jacob and Laban.* The relationships between the patriarch and Laban the Aramean take place in Upper Mesopotamia, in Haran, the city which Abraham had departed to enter Canaan. The story begins with Jacob meeting Laban's daughter Rachel at a well near Haran. With that introduction Jacob entered his uncle's household and worked for a month (29:1–14).

When the question about wages came up, Jacob agreed to work for seven years in return for the hand of the beautiful and lovely Rachel. When the contractual period had passed, the festive evening wedding took place. But when Jacob awoke in the light of the following morning, he discovered he had married Leah instead. Then Laban explained to the enraged Jacob that it was not the custom to give in marriage the younger daughter before the firstborn (*bᵉkîrâ*, 29:26; note the play on Jacob's acquisition of his brother's *bᵉkōrâ* at 25:29–34). Thus "the cheater" has been cheated! But in order to restore some semblance of peaceful relations, Laban promised that in one week Jacob could marry Rachel also—in return for another seven years of service (29:27–30). Through two wives and their maidservants Jacob watched his family grow to a dozen sons and one daughter. The way to becoming a nation was clear. God was acting in the midst of all the human treachery and deception to fulfill his repeated promises.

After the birth of Joseph, Jacob raised with Laban the possibility of his returning home with his growing family. As payment for services rendered, Jacob proposed to settle for the blemished sheep and goats and for the black lambs among Laban's flocks (30:25–34). But in another attempt to cheat the patriarch, Laban removed all such animals from the flock and kept them at a safe distance from Jacob (vv. 35–36). Not to be outdone again, Jacob devised a scheme by which he blemished every strong animal in the flocks, and "thus the man grew exceedingly rich" (30:37–43). Like Abraham (Gen. 12:16, 20; 20:14) and Isaac (Gen. 26:13–14) before him, Jacob became wealthy after an act of deception. Yet far from serving as a prescription on "how to get rich quick," each story attests that the prosperity of the patriarch is due to the intervention, blessing, and presence of God even in the midst of manipulations of his own chosen people (12:17; 20:6; 26:12; 31:5, 42).

Finally, with wealth acquired Jacob was commanded by God to return home—a rare appearance of the deity in this Jacob tradition. And so Jacob stole away from his uncle and father-in-law Laban with all that the patriarch had acquired in Haran. Unknown to Jacob, however, was a possession in the caravan which was not his: Laban's household gods which Rachel had stolen. When Laban had learned of the flight, he pursued the caravan in order to find his gods.

This episode leads to the conclusion of the Jacob-Laban story. At 31:43–55 the two adversaries made a covenant, swearing to do no harm to the other in front of "the heap of witness." They concluded the covenant by eating together (cf. 26:28–30), and Laban left for home after giving his blessing to his daughters and grandchildren. This final episode is considered by Martin Noth to be the origin of the entire Jacob-Laban tradition: a treaty made between the Israelites of Gilead and their Aramean neighbors at a certain boundary line (31:52) dividing pasture grounds and watering holes (*History of Pentateuchal Traditions*, pp. 91–94).

3. *The theophanies.* Interspersed throughout the Jacob cycle are several stories in which God appears to the patriarch at particular sites. One such story at 32:1–2 records that the angels of God appeared to Jacob as an army, and so he called the place Mahanaim. Though brief, the record does help confirm the presence of Jacob traditions east of the Jordan in the land of Gilead.

More important as an East Jordanian site for a theophany to Jacob is the story about Peniel at Genesis 32:22–32. The story records essentially that because a god named El appeared during the night to wrestle with the patriarch, a cultic sanctuary named Peniel/Penuel had its origin. Inserted into the cultic legend, however, are two other aetiologies: the explanation for the dietary taboo, and the origin of the name Israel.

The first of these aetiologies is unknown elsewhere in the Old Testament. The second is more common but difficult to interpret. Does the new name indicate a change as such in the personality of the man, recognizing that the name for the ancient Semites was more a matter of identity than of identification? Or is the new name a means of equating a Jacob and an Israel who were originally independent of each other as two persons, or as two groups of clans? The Priest's record of the name change from Jacob to Israel at 35:9–10 does not really help the interpreter to decide on the original meaning. In its present context, however, the story seems to stress the change in the character of Jacob. As "the cheater" was about to face his brother Esau (Gen. 33) for the first time since the deception, God intervened to enable the patriarch to take the role of a humble servant rather than a conniving rascal. Thus the Peniel episode seems to have been inserted secondarily into the story by someone who intended to explain the changed relationship between Jacob and Esau (see McCurley, *Promise,* pp. 84–92, 151–155).

The theophany at Genesis 28:10–22 likewise is related directly to a cultic place: Bethel. This theophany account intrudes into the narrative as a transition piece between the stories of Jacob and Esau and those about Jacob and Laban, just as the Peniel theophany occurred as Jacob traveled from Laban to Esau. In its present form the story is a combination of two sources: J and E. The Elohist's account at verses 11–12, 17–18, and possibly 20–22 tells of the founding of the sanctuary at Bethel. Like the Tower of Babel (Gen. 11:1–9) and the oak at Shechem (Judg. 9:3), the site here is a "navel of the earth." The ramp on which the angels of God ascended and descended marks the spot as the holy place of intercourse between the divine and earthly worlds. The reinterpretation of this phenomenon at John 1:51 is particularly interesting. There the ascending and descending of the angels of God takes place not at a certain site but on a particular person: the Son of Man. Thus holiness is transferred from sacred places to the person of Jesus Christ.

Into the cultic aetiological legend of E the redactor who combined J and E set the introduction and speech of Yahweh from the J source (vv. 13–14). "I am the Lord . . ." introduces Yahweh to Jacob for the first time. In this first encounter, as in the case of Abraham and Isaac, the Lord announced his promise of land and descendants and reiterated the kerygmatic formula: "and by you and your descendants shall all the families of the land consider themselves blessed" (v. 14). How appropriate that the formula occurs as Jacob was on his way to live among Arameans with whom the patriarch ultimately made a covenant of peace (cf. the covenant which Isaac made with Abimelech after the formula was addressed to him, Gen. 26).

Added to that customary set of promises is a new one: "I will be with you and will protect you wherever you go, and I will bring you back to this land; for I will not forsake you until I have done that of which I have spoken to you" (v. 15). The verse is usually assigned to J along with verses 13–14, and from the story line there is no reason to reject that view. It is interesting, however, that in the midst of an otherwise stereotyped set of formulas from J (vv. 13–14), verse 15 contains one expression after another which is nowhere else used by the Yahwist. The combination of "I will be with you" with "on all the way that you go" occurs, however, at Joshua 1:9, and with "I will not forsake you" at Deuteronomy 31:6, 8; Joshua 1:5—all texts from the Deuteronomistic editor of the exilic period. Moreover, the promise "I will bring you back" is common in the prose sections of the Book of Jeremiah which also addresses exiles and would-be exiles in the sixth century B.C. (see Jer. 12:15; 16:15; 23:3, etc.) Thus it seems likely that the promise to Jacob of God's presence, protection, and return is an insertion into the Yahweh speech in order to address exiles in the sixth century B.C. with the message that just as the Lord was faithful in those promises to Jacob, so he will be faithful to them in Babylon.

In that light the response of Jacob in verses 20–22 might likewise represent an exilic supplement. Again, while nothing in substance eliminates the vow from the E source, the terminology throughout has parallels only in the Deuteronomistic history and in other late texts. The closest parallel to our own text in content and form is the vow of Absalom at 2 Samuel 15:7-8 (cf. also 1 Sam. 1:11; Judg. 11:30, 39). Interestingly, the vow formula is connected to tithing elsewhere only at Deuteronomy 12:17. If this speech of Jacob in verses 20–22 is likewise intended for exiles of a later time, then the meaning seems to lie in the appropriate response of Israel to God's promises of presence, protection, and return.

According to the Elohist, Jacob returned to the site of his dream at the command of God that he and his household leave Shechem in order to dwell at Bethel (Gen. 35:1-8). Like the later Israelites under Joshua (Josh. 24:14, 23), Jacob's group "put away the foreign gods which are among you" at the Shechem sanctuary (Gen. 35:2-4). When they arrived at Bethel, Jacob built an altar to God who had appeared to him at that place earlier (28:11-12, 17-18) and called the place El-bethel (v. 7). According to Martin Noth, this story reflects the transferral of Jacob traditions from their original home at Shechem to the sanctuary at Bethel and is linked cultically to an old celebration of a "pilgrimage from Shechem to Bethel" (see *History of Pentateuchal Traditions,* pp. 80f.).

In any case, there is attached to this E narrative another Bethel revelation—this one recorded by P at 35:9-15. It is in Bethel, according to this story, not at Peniel, where God changed Jacob's name to Israel. Immediately, God introduced himself to Jacob—for the first time in the Priestly narrative—as El Shaddai, the name given to Abraham at Genesis 17:1. Moreover, the promises of fruitfulness and land were given to Jacob as to Abraham earlier, including that kerygmatic Priestly formula "be fruitful and multiply" (35:11). In fact, the Priest explicitly connects Jacob with Abraham and Isaac in the promise of the land. On the basis of this revelation, Jacob called the place Bethel (v. 15).

According to the Yahwist, the Elohist, and the Priest, God revealed himself first to Jacob at Bethel. In the Elohist's version at Genesis 28:11ff. the promise of land and descendants entered into the theophany by the merging with J's typical formula of divine introduction and promises (vv. 13-14). The Priest accomplished on his own the combination of revelation of name and the giving of promises at 35:9-15. Thus the entire story, as we have it, consisting of such separate traditions as Jacob and Esau, Jacob and Laban, and several theophanies, is held together by the appearances and promises of God to Jacob at the site of Bethel. Even the kerygmatic formulas of the Yahwist (28:14) and of the Priest (35:11) are applied to Jacob at Bethel, the framework site.

There is no better evidence for the power of God's word in promise and fulfillment than this entire story of Jacob. Even to "the cheater" par excellence, the fugitive on the run, God continued his commitment of land, descendants, and blessing which he began with Abraham. Moreover, in the movement of the entire story, Jacob separated himself from the land, but God intervened in order to restore him (cf. Gen. 12:10–20). Again, when man is the subject, the result of the action is alienation. Only when the subject is God does the story end in restoration.

THE PATRIARCHS AND THEIR RELIGION

During the past three decades few issues in Old Testament scholarship have aroused as much interest as the patriarchs. Scholars have been studying and debating the dates for Abraham, Isaac, and Jacob, their importance for specific groups who later became Israel, their relationships to one another, their religion, and the methodologies employed to deal with these questions. On the question of dating the patriarchs and their relationships to one another, the reader will benefit from the survey by the late Roland deVaux in *The Early History of Israel* (pp. 161–166). For an evaluation of methodologies in patriarchal study, the reader is referred to two works which raise questions about the methods used heretofore: van Seters, *Abraham in History and Tradition,* and Thompson, *The Historicity of the Patriarchal Narratives.* Space permits here only a discussion of the religion of the patriarchs and the significance of their faith for understanding the tradition of God's promises.

A major issue to consider is the name of the God whom the patriarchs worshiped. It is no accident that two of the three Tetrateuchal sources avoid the name Yahweh in the Book of Genesis. Only the Yahwist source employs the Tetragrammaton YHWH from the very beginning; when Enosh was born to Seth, people began to "call upon the name of Yahweh" (Gen. 4:26). The Priest, however, throughout the prehistory in Genesis 1—11, uses "God" (Heb. *'elōhîm*) for the deity, and in the patriarchal stories he generally employs *El Shaddai* (Gen. 17 and 35 particularly). The Elohist, not evident in Genesis 1—11, uses *'elōhîm* consistently through the patriarchal narratives. Thus two sources in Genesis 12—50 reflect the view that the patriarchs called God something other than Yahweh.

The pioneering work in this area was done in 1929 by Albrecht Alt. His study "Der Gott der Väter" which now appears in English in the collection *Essays on Old Testament History and Religion* (pp. 1–100) is accepted widely among Old Testament scholars. Generally, his thesis is that the patriarchs brought with them into Canaan a religion best described as "god of the father" worship. Not tied to any particular sanctuary, the god was thus a nomadic deity who promised protection, land, and descendants. "God the father" is used with the possessive pronouns "my," "your," "his" before "father" at Genesis 31:5; 43:23; 46:3; 50:17. More often the god is referred to by the name of the father: the God of Abraham (26:24; 28:13; 31:53; 32:9), the God of Isaac (28:13; 32:9; 46:1), the God of Nahor (31:53). The merging of originally separate groups of people is attested when two or more names of patriarchs appear: "God of my father Abraham and God of my father Isaac" (32:9), "the God of Abraham your father and the God of Isaac" (28:13), and "the God of Abraham, the God of Isaac, and the God of Jacob" (Exod. 3:6, 15; cf. also v. 16). By these combinations the originally separate deities became identified as one and the same. Occasionally, a specific name is given to the deity: "Fear of Isaac" (Gen. 31:42, 53) or "the Mighty One of Jacob" (49:24–25). (The "shield" of Abraham at Genesis 15:1 seems to be more of a metaphor than a title.)

As the patriarchs entered Canaan with their nomadic deities, they encountered at specific sanctuaries veneration of the god El. The biblical texts themselves attest to this encounter with the chief god of the Canaanite pantheon whom we know especially from the Ugaritic texts of the fifteenth to the twelfth centuries B.C. At Beerlahai-roi where Isaac lived at first (25:11), Hagar addressed *El Roi* ("El who sees") as she fled from Sarah (16:13–14). At Beer-sheba where both Abraham and Isaac lived, Abraham worshiped *El Olam* ("El the Eternal," 21:33). At Bethel, the center of Jacob traditions, that patriarch anointed a pillar and later built an altar to *El Bethel*

("El of Bethel," 31:13; 35:7); there is some evidence that Bethel is the name of a god and not simply a place (cf. Jer. 48:13 and perhaps Zech. 7:2). Also at Bethel, according to P, the deity introduced himself to Jacob as *El Shaddai* ("El the Mountain" or "El of the Mountain," 35:11; 48:3); however this name is not so tied to a sanctuary as are the others (see 17:1; 43:14; 49:25). Finally, there is *El Elyon* ("God Most High") who blesses Abraham and who receives the patriarch's tithe (14:18–20); *Elyon* seems to be the revelation of El at Jerusalem (for Salem as Jerusalem see Ps. 76:2) for whom Melchizedek, the king, was priest (cf. Ps. 110:4).

Thus the god El, whom we know from Ugarit as the "father of mankind," "the creator of creatures," and as the head of a heavenly court, was incorporated into the worship of the "god of the father" religions which the patriarchs brought with them into Canaan. El, the god of a sedentary civilization, was the rightful owner of the land, as his sanctuaries all over the land confirmed. By identifying the god of their respective fathers who promised land and descendants with El, the owner of the land, the Hebrews could look with confidence on the fulfillment of the promises. To further identify from the very beginning this El of the patriarchs with Yahweh, the J writer of the tenth century B.C. was confessing that Yahweh, the God of Israel, was the one who was faithful to the promises he had made to Abraham, Isaac, and Jacob. How appropriate that in the J source El, the father of humanity, is one and the same as Yahweh, the God who is concerned ultimately with the blessing for all the families of the land!

CHAPTER FIVE

ENTRY AND THE NEW PROMISE

Scattered throughout the Deuteronomistic corpus from Deuteronomy through Kings are several historical surveys which Gerhard von Rad has labeled "historical credos" (see *The Problem of the Hexateuch and Other Essays,* pp. 1–17). Most striking of the various examples is the one incorporated into a rite for offering the firstfruits of the harvest at Deuteronomy 26:1–11.

A WANDERING ARAMEAN WAS MY FATHER;
> *he went down* to Egypt and sojourned there with people small in number;
> and there he became a great nation (*gôy gādôl*), strong and many,
> and the Egyptians treated us with evil and afflicted us
>> and set on us hard labor.

Then we cried out to Yahweh, God of our fathers.
AND YAHWEH HEARD OUR VOICE,
> and saw our affliction and our toil and our pain.

And *Yahweh brought us out* from Egypt
> with a strong hand and outstretched arm,
> and with a great miracle and with signs and wonders.

And *he brought us in* to this place,
> and he gave to us this land,
> a land flowing with milk and honey (Deut. 26:5–9; emphasis added).

Several themes stand out in the structure of this confession which seems to consists of two stanzas. (1) The subjects of the first part are "my father" and "we." Their action led to trouble: harsh treatment by the Egyptians to whose land the father "went down." (2) The subject of the second part is Yahweh, identified in a transition between the two parts as the "God of our fathers." With God as actor, the direction changes. He *brought* the people *out* of Egypt in order to *bring* them *into* the Promised Land. Thus, once again, as in the Abraham story at Genesis 12:10–20 and in the entire Jacob cycle, when the subject of the action in regard to land is the patriarch, the result is separation from the land; when the subject is the Lord, the result is restoration to the land.

The major themes of the little confessional history of Deuteronomy 26:5–9 are strikingly consistent with those in similar confessions at Deuteronomy 6:20–24; 1 Samuel 12:8; and Joshua 24:2–13. Moreover, these major themes of the fathers going down to Egypt, the change of subject to Yahweh, and then Yahweh's bringing the people out of Egypt, are the topics of elaborate narratives ranging from Genesis 37—Exodus 15. Either as earlier outlines of later narratives (von Rad) or later summaries of earlier narratives (Vriezen and others), the little statements provide the scheme for our discussion in this chapter and the next.

ENTRANCE INTO EGYPT

The so-called "Joseph story" is introduced in the Bible by the Priest as "the history of the family of Jacob" (37:2). It is clear, however, that the major figure in the family is Joseph, introduced as a lad of seventeen years who is his father's favorite son, the firstborn through beloved Rachel. The unpopularity of Joseph among his brothers is attested by his tattletale ways (37:2), his father's favoritism, evidenced by the gift of the long-sleeved robe (37:3), and his wild-eyed dreams about ruling over the rest of them (37:5–11). With rampant rivalry so clear at the beginning of the story, it comes as no surprise when the brothers "conspired against him to kill him" (37:18), as he approached them at the pasture near Dothan. Convinced by Reuben at one point (v. 22) and Judah at another (v. 26), the brothers decided not to kill him but to sell him to a caravan of Ishmaelites (vv. 25, 28b), according to one writer, and to Midianites (vv. 28a, 36), according to another. In either case Joseph ended up in Egypt (vv. 28, 36).

Despite some inconsistencies and duplications of details, the Joseph story cannot be fragmented into smaller units. Attempts at separation of the long story into sources have not been fruitful, for after the introductory chapter (37), sources are no longer clearly distinguishable. (Even the divine name Elohim occurs in passages traditionally assigned to the Yahwist.) Nor is the story a collection of sagas, like the cycles of Abraham and Jacob. Rather, "it is from beginning to end an organically constructed narrative" (von Rad, *Genesis,* p. 347). While such a conclusion does not rule out the possibility of earlier sources or levels of supplementation, the text of the Joseph story is so masterfully composed that the narrative is best treated as a whole (see the literary work by Coats, *From Canaan to Egypt*).

In its entirety, the Joseph story is generally classified as a "novella," a story about an individual who must come to terms with the human society around him/her. The background of such a story gives the impression of a unique event but the story itself can occur over and over. The conclusion of a novella is oriented toward a solution of the individual's dilemma. In this classification, the Joseph story is similar to the Book of Ruth, to the framework of the Job story, and particularly to the Book of Esther.

In 1953 Gerhard von Rad demonstrated that the Joseph story is best understood in terms of old wisdom. As in such wisdom books as Job and Proverbs, there is in the Joseph story no interest in cultic matters, in national pride, or in covenant theology. Moreover, on the basis of qualities outlined in those wisdom books and others, Joseph, with a position in the vicinity of the king, appears as a wise man in Genesis 37—50. On the basis of his "fear of God" which is the beginning of wisdom (Prov. 1:17; 15:33), Joseph is the model of breeding, education, modesty, knowledge, and self-control (see the Book of Proverbs). This same fear of God prevented Joseph from succumbing to the seductive advances of Potiphar's wife (cf. Prov. 22:14; 23:27f.). Furthermore, Joseph manages to keep a cool head in the face of his brothers (see Prov. 10:19; 12:23; 14:29, 30; 16:32) and heeds the admonition against hatred (Prov. 10:12; 24:29).

While arguments have been raised against von Rad's position, the main lines of his thesis seem to stand firm—particularly in light of the framework of the story. According to wisdom teaching, the truly wise man knows his limitations in the face of God's superior wisdom. "Many are the plans in the mind of a man, but it is the purpose of the

Lord that will be established" (Prov. 19:21; see also 16:9; 20:24). Even the Egyptian Book of Amen-em-opet teaches that "One thing are the words which men say, Another is that which the god does" (Chapter 18, *ANET*, p. 423). Likewise the Joseph story begins with the evil plans of the brothers who "conspired against him to kill him" (37:18) and ends with a double statement that God made it work out for good: to preserve life.

The first of these statements occurs at Genesis 45:1–8. The scene in which Joseph revealed to his brothers his true identity as the long-lost dreamer is filled with emotional outburst. Immediately after his disclosure "I am Joseph," he consoled his brothers about their foul deed of years past with the announcement that "God sent me before you to preserve life" (v. 5) and further "God sent me before you to preserve for you a remnant on earth, and to keep alive for you many survivors. So it was not you who sent me here, but God" (vv. 7–8a).

The second passage to round out the wisdom teaching is Genesis 50:15–21. After the death of Jacob in Egypt, the brothers plotted again—this time for Joseph's forgiveness. They told him his father's dying wish was that Joseph forgive their transgression. Again Joseph wept, and again he comforted them with the news that God had already acted to incorporate their transgression into his plan of preserving life. "You devised evil against me, but God devised it for good, to the effect that many people should be kept alive, as they are today" (v. 20). As Joseph dreamed at the beginning that his brothers would bow down to him (37:9), so indeed they did at the end (50:18). But God's purpose of it all was to transform their conspiracy to kill (37:18) into his plan to save life (50:20). Again, as in the teaching of Proverbs, God has had the last word!

The Joseph story, therefore, seems indeed to have been composed as an independent novella primarily to educate in the wisdom of God. Originally it seems to have had little—if anything—to do with the patriarchal traditions of Genesis. Apparently, it was composed and circulated among the wisdom teachers who lived in the territory of "the house of Joseph," that is, in central Palestine.

The incorporation of the story into the history of God's saving activity with his people gives it a new function. It serves now to explain how it happened that the ancestors of Israel were living in Egypt. Thus, it is a transition from the patriarchal stories to the exodus event. It looks back to make the connection with Jacob ("the history of the family of Jacob," 37:2) who left home in time of famine to visit Beer-sheba and offer sacrifices to "the God of his father Isaac (46:1ff.). The transitional story, however, primarily looks forward to the departure from Egypt, for God promised "I will go down with you to Egypt, and I will also bring you up again" (46:4). Moreover, the additions to the end of the story make the promise even more explicit: Joseph's last words were "I am about to die; but God will visit you, and bring you up out of this land to the land which he swore to Abraham, to Isaac, and to Jacob" (50:24). This is the only occurrence of the divine promise in the entire Joseph story, but its climactic effect binds together the promise given and the fulfillment to be realized.

Our immediate concern is to flesh out the confessional statement that in Egypt the wandering father became "a great nation (*gôy gādôl*), strong and many" (Deut. 26:5). The promise given to Abraham at Genesis 12:2, that the Lord would make him "a great nation" (*gôy gādôl*), comes to fulfillment in the Priest's own transition at Exodus 1:1–7. The seventy offspring of Jacob's family who went down to Egypt experienced the promised blessing of God that they be fruitful and multiply (Exod. 1:7; cf. Gen. 17:6; 35:11).

The realization of that divine blessing, however, led to near disaster, because the growing numbers led the new pharaoh "who did not know Joseph" to subject the people with the heavy burden of building royal cities (Exod. 1:8–14). The cities the people built were Pithom and Raamses (Exod. 1:11). Pithom has been identified as the site Pr-Itm, "the house of Atum." The city, located in the eastern end of the Wadi-Tumilat, seems to have been built by Rameses II in the thirteenth century B.C. The city of Raamses has been identified as Pr-R'mssw-mry-'Imn, "the House of Rameses, the beloved of Amun" and thus located in the northeastern delta. The city is obviously connected to the building activity of Rameses II and, like Pithom, helps to date the subjection of the Hebrews during his reign in the thirteenth century B.C.

The description of the oppression itself in Exodus 1:8–12 (J) and 1:13–14 (P) seems therefore to reflect historical reminiscence and is repeated throughout the Old Testament. That the Elohist's description in 1:15–22 is both illogical (it describes the destruction of a generation of slaves) and unique (attested nowhere else in the Old Testament) has led Brevard Childs to conclude that it was composed as a literary explanation for the motive of exposing to danger the infant Moses (2:1–10). (See "The Birth of Moses," pp. 109ff.) The story about the instruction to slaughter the baby boys sets the tone of the oppression at an even higher level: now at stake is the future of the Hebrew people, for their extermination at the order of the Egyptian king seems inevitable. It remains for the Hebrew midwives who "feared God" to disobey the order and "to preserve life" for the male children (cf. the Joseph story discussed above). Foiled in his clever scheme by the Hebrew midwives, Pharaoh issues the same order to all his people, and the stage is thus set for the unfolding drama.

Enter Moses! In the infancy story of 2:1–10 Moses is introduced as a Hebrew baby who became the adopted son of the Pharaoh's daughter. The story, as a unit, has been identified by Childs as a wisdom tale on the basis of its peculiar Hebrew features which are attached to an old wet-nurse contract formula. Most scholars have drawn parallels to other ancient exposure legends, particularly "The Legend of Sargon" (*ANET*, p. 119). Whatever the form-critical background of the story, the account does point to the work of divine providence (without mentioning God) in the context of the oppression of the Hebrews. At the same time it introduces the person whom God will use to accomplish his will.

The man Moses, whose name is as Egyptian as that of Rameses ("son of Ra"), is identified in infancy as a Hebrew: a Levite, a suckling of a Hebrew woman. As a young man Moses again is portrayed as a Hebrew who kills an Egyptian beating "one of his people" (2:11–15). In addition to identifying Moses, the story serves to move Moses from Egypt to Midian (v. 15b). Now Moses became related to Midianites—by marriage to the daughter of the priest of Midian with whom he dwelled and in whose territory he met Yahweh.

YAHWEH, MOSES, AND THE NEW PROMISE

The J writer used the name Yahweh from the very beginning of his story—at creation itself—and explicitly stated that from the time of Seth's son Enosh, "men began to call upon the name of Yahweh" (Gen. 4:26). The Elohist and the Priest, however, studiously avoided the name Yahweh until it was given to Moses. The two accounts of this revelation, that of the Elohist at Exodus 3:13–15 and that of the Priest at Exodus 6:2–3, deserve particular attention.

According to E, the name-giving event is set within the context of the call and commission of Moses at Exodus 3:1–12 (or in the expanded form at 3:1—4:17). While the commissioning itself has been sharply separated into two sources (J at 3:1ab, 2–4a, 5, 7–8; E at 3:1c, 4b, 6, 9–12), the text should be interpreted as a basic unit. Examining the text in this way leads to the conviction that its form is that of a call narrative, most similar to the call of Gideon at Judges 6:11–24 and of Jeremiah at Jeremiah 1:4–10 (see Childs, *Book of Exodus,* pp. 52–56). It is in relationship to this commissioning as a deliverer that Moses asked the question of God, "If I come to the people of Israel and say to them, 'The God of your fathers (see v. 6) has sent me to you,' and they ask me 'what is his name?' What shall I say to them?"

At first glance Moses' question seems to be a clever attempt to learn the name of the deity who confronted him. On other occasions in the Old Testament, such a question was left unanswered. Jacob simply blurted out "Tell me your name" (Gen. 32:29), and Manoah, with a bit more finesse, said "What is your name, so that, when your words come true, we may honor you?" (Judg. 13:17). Neither one of those men received an answer to the question; in fact, in each case the divine being disappeared immediately. Now Moses placed the issue squarely in the mouths of the enslaved Hebrews who will ask "what is his name?" And with uncharacteristic abandon God answered:

> Say this to the people of Israel:
>> Yahweh, the God of your fathers,
>>> the God of Abraham, the God of Isaac, and the God
>>> of Jacob,
>> has sent me to you.
>> This is my name forever,
>>> and this is my designation for all generations (3:15;
>>> author's translation).

The Elohist thus records that God revealed his name Yahweh to Moses on Mt. Horeb (alias Sinai) in the context of the commissioning formula. Further, he explicitly identifies Yahweh as one and the

same as the God of the fathers who gave the promises to the patriarchs. Thus while continuity with the past is stressed in verses 6 and
15, at the same time the new name Yahweh begins a new era in God's
relationships. Previously God revealed himself to individuals: the
patriarchs. Now he reveals himself through an individual (Moses) to
a people, Israel, whose oppression in Egypt he has seen.

It seems that the famous paranomastic expression "I am who I
am" in verse 14 is a later insertion into the text. It interrupts the flow
from Moses' question in verse 13 to God's answer in verse 15. Moreover, the repetition of "Say this to the people of Israel" in verses 14
and 15 seems to reflect the presence of two hands at the pen rather
than one. J. P. Hyatt argues that the addition was made in the seventh
or sixth centuries B.C. when monotheism was being debated, and so
to settle the debate an editor inserted this verse in order to express,
"I am the one truly existent deity" (*JBL* 86 [1967] 369–377). Certainly the insertion of such a mysterious expression "I am who I am"
removed any pretense of ability to control the deity. Further, the formula seems to provide an intentional connection with the commissioning of Moses: in verse 12 God assured the man of his presence
with the declarative "I will be with you" (*'ehyeh 'immāk*); now, it
seems, as a follow-up to that pledge God said first "I am/will be who
I am/will be" (*'ehyeh *'*ašer 'ehyeh*). One might even consider the
possibility that verse 14 was formulated as it was only because of the
earlier pledge of divine presence; in verse 12 it must be primary because of the commissioning formula (cf. Judg. 6:16).

That the matter is not quite so easily solved can be seen in the
attention Exodus 3:14 has received among scholars. Some have tried
to analyze the name Yahweh and its explanation here on the basis of
a Hebrew word "to fall" (*hw'*), and to extend the meaning to falling
of rain or lightning or enemies. Others connect Yahweh with an
Arabic word "to blow" (*hawaya*) and so interpret God as a storm
god. Particularly interesting from a theological point of view is the
suggestion that the root is the Ugaritic *hwt* ("word"; Akkadian
awatu), and thus Yahweh is one who reveals himself in a word; unfortunately the philological evidence for this suggestion is no better
than the others. More impressive are the arguments that the name
Yahweh points to a creator deity (see Freedman, *JBL* 79 [1960]
151–156; Cross, *HTR* 55 [1962] 225–259). Finally, study of the

recently discovered Ebla tablets has led one of the chief investigators to argue that the short form *Ya* (attested frequently in the Old Testament) appears in personal names alternately with El; further, after the reign of Eblaite King Ebrum (connected with biblical Eber, Gen. 11:15–16, whose name is sometimes considered to be the origin of "Hebrew") *Ya* is consistently substituted for El. Thus it is argued that under Ebrum in the twenty-fourth or -third centuries B.C., Ya came to the fore as a new development took place in West Semitic religions (see Pettinato, *BA* 39 [1976] 48).

Such confusion leads the interpreter to experience relief in the fact that faith or even understanding the biblical witnesses to the faith, is not based upon etymological explanations. It seems that we do not know precisely what the name Yahweh means or where and when and how it originated. If the insertion of the paranomastic expression at Exodus 3:14 was at all intended as a means of expressing the mystery of the name, modern scholarship has confirmed that purpose precisely by trying to explain the verse. What is more important in the story is the function and explanation of the name in light of the commission to Moses and the purpose of God. Since the Priestly writer uses the name revelation in essentially the same way as the Elohist, we shall turn to Exodus 6:2–3 for a brief discussion before returning to the question of function.

Thus far in the Book of Exodus, the Priest has recorded the growth of the people from small numbers to a great multitude (1:1–7), the forced labor of the people at the hands of the Egyptians (1:13–14), and the groaning of the enslaved people to God who heard their cry for help and "remembered his covenant with Abraham, with Isaac, and with Jacob" (2:23–24). Just as God remembered Noah (Gen. 8:1) and so transformed the chaos of the primeval flood into a new beginning of life and order (Gen. 9), so now he remembers the covenant with the patriarchs in which he promised descendants, land, and relationship with himself. The situation again borders on destruction of life, and so once again God must act to restore his order and fulfill his promises.

In this setting occurs the revelation of the name Yahweh to Moses. For the Priest the event took place not on Mt. Horeb but in Egypt, an idea which seems to predate the exilic theologian (cf. Hos. 12:9; 13:4). Once again, the name-giving relates Yahweh to the patriarchal god but at the same time marks a sharp contrast to the former revelations (Gen. 17:1; 28:3; 35:11).

> I am Yahweh.
> I appeared to Abraham, to Isaac, and to Jacob as El Shaddai,
>   but by my name Yahweh I did not make myself known to them
>   (Exod. 6:2–3).

The Lord continued his announcement by explicitly connecting the covenant promise of land to the patriarchs with the new promise that he will deliver the people from their bondage and "take you as my people" (vv. 7–8). The accomplishment of that historical event of redemption will be the revelation to all the people that "I am Yahweh your God." This particular formula which bases knowledge of Yahweh on his saving acts occurs more than seventy times in the preaching of that other exilic priest, Ezekiel (e.g., Ezek. 13:23; 37:6, 14). While Abraham, Jacob, and Moses learned of God through his self-disclosure in direct address, the people of Israel and others too will learn who he is on the basis of his saving activity for Israel (see the occurrence of the formula in the Priest's account of the sea event at Exod. 14:18). Here the divine name Yahweh was given to Moses in the context of the new promise of deliverance and of the continuing promise of land. The fulfillments have not yet occurred, and so the people have not yet come to the knowledge of God (6:9).

Thus, in spite of different settings, the Priest and the Elohist recorded the revelation of the Yahweh name to Israel through Moses. The significance of the event is deeper than the mere words convey. In the ancient world the name of a person was far more than a matter of identification—as it is for us today; the name had more to do with identity. For this reason we can understand why Jacob and Manoah wanted so desperately to learn the name of the deity: they could virtually have a "genie in the lamp." For the same reason we can see why the deity left each of those men without giving a name: God did not wish to be controlled. To Moses, however, God gave his name Yahweh without any strings attached.

Why would God take such a risk of being controlled—not only by Moses but by all the people of Israel to whom the name would be announced? Only for one reason: the salvation of his people was at stake, the promises to Abraham were in danger! And so God took the risk, just as he did when he passed between the parts of the dissected animals to guarantee his promise of land (Gen. 15:7–21).

Before leaving this section, it is important to give some attention to the Yahwist's story at this point. Again, the elements of the commissioning formula occupy almost all of 3:1–12. It is difficult to determine what—if anything except verses 7–8—belongs to the J source. Whether or not the Yahwist told of the burning bush episode, whether or not the bush was originally the "sign" of verse 12 which was moved forward in the story as an attention-getting device (see the discussion in Childs, *Book of Exodus,* pp. 56–60), the bush serves little theological purpose for J in its present location. What is important is that Moses was addressed by the Lord with an assurance of salvation (3:7–8). The Yahwist's story continues at 3:16–17 where the Lord instructed Moses to announce the divine promise that God would take the people out of Egypt to the Promised Land.

While the Yahwist has no special event announcing the Yahweh name to Moses and while for him the name does not begin a new era, nevertheless this theologian too connects the God of the patriarchs to Yahweh in the context of the new promise to deliver as a means of fulfilling the old promise of land. That land itself is described by him as "a good and broad land," a designation which seems to convey in itself the promise of deliverance from bondage (cf. Job 36:16; Ps. 18:19).

It is in the role of Moses that the Yahwist differs from the Elohist. For E Moses was sent to "bring forth the children of Israel out of Egypt" (3:10–11); he was a deliverer, as was Gideon (see his call narrative at Judg. 6:14; *hôšaʿtā* = "you shall save"). But in the Yahwist's record at verses 7–8, 16–17, the deliverer was exclusively Yahweh: "I have come down to deliver them." What Moses is to do, according to J, is simply to announce to the people the inevitability of Yahweh's act of deliverance: "go and gather the elders of Israel and say to them . . ." (v. 16).

YAHWEH AND THE PATRIARCHAL GOD

All three sources equate Yahweh with "the God of the fathers" or with El Shaddai who was worshiped by the patriarchs. Moreover, all three make this equation in the combination of the old land promise with the new salvation promise. Just as the exodus was related to land at Genesis 15:13–16, so in Exodus 3 and 6 the land is related to the deliverance from bondage. Finally, for all three sources the mediator of the name and of the new promise is Moses.

It seems the religion of Moses introduced Yahweh into the El worship of the patriarchs and eventually Yahweh and El were identified. In the Old Testament itself various stages of this development are attested. One stage seems to be represented in those texts which acknowledge El as superior to Yahweh: Deuteronomy 32:8–9 tells that when Elyon, the chief of the pantheon, distributed the peoples of the earth to "the sons of El" Yahweh was assigned the people of Jacob. Other texts hint that El is at least separate from Yahweh (Gen. 14:18–24; Isa. 14:13). Another stage is the deliberate and emphatic attempt to identify El and Yahweh, especially in Second Isaiah (Isa. 40:18; 43:12; 45:22). Still another stage is the rather casual use of El as a designation of Yahweh (Josh. 22:22: Ps. 104; Job 3:1—42:5). All this enables us to understand that while there is constant polemic in the Old Testament against Baal, never is El considered a rival to Yahweh.

The identification with El brought to Yahweh some important characteristics: king over a heavenly court (cf. Isa. 6:1–8; 1 Kings 22:19–23; Job 1), the function of Creator (cf. Ps. 95, esp. vv. 3–5), perhaps even concern for the poor and needy (Prov. 22:22–23; 23:10–11). At the same time El acquired a new role in the identification, that of deliverer: El brought Israel out of Egypt (Num. 23:22; 24:8). This identification probably took place during the settlement in the land as clans and tribes merged, but it surely was cemented when David took over Jerusalem and adopted, it seems, many of the customs and some of the religion of the Jebusites who worshiped El/Elyon (Gen. 14:18–24; Ps. 46:4; cf. Ps. 110:4).

Whatever the details of this later relationship, Yahweh made himself known through Moses in a startling way: he revealed his name. Yet, as we know from a cross on Golgotha, no risk is too great for God when the salvation of his people is at stake.

CHAPTER SIX

DEPARTURE AND CONFESSION

The old confessional formula at Deuteronomy 26:8 describes the deliverance from Egypt with striking brevity: "And Yahweh brought us out from Egypt with a strong hand and outstretched arm, and with a great miracle and with signs and wonders." Apart from the mention of strength and wonderful acts, the record tells us nothing about the means and method which the Lord used to accomplish the departure. Yet even the brief record in this one verse points to some dramatic event.

The drama which unfolds in Exodus 1—15 is nothing less than a contest between two gods: Yahweh, the God of the Hebrew slaves, and Pharaoh, the god of Egypt. The ruler of Egypt was considered to be the god Horus who ruled the land from the royal throne; at death the pharaoh became the god Osiris. Seen in this light, the repeated formula "Let my people go, that they may serve me" takes on particular meaning: Let my people go from serving you, god of Egypt, that they may serve me, God of Israel. Indeed, by understanding the Pharaoh as the god of Egypt, the story has particular impact: Yahweh against a mere human is no contest. (Although by that alignment of forces, the story does qualify as a comedy; see Robertson, *The Old Testament and the Literary Critic.*)

Thus the issue at stake is not simply a sociological enslavement but a theological bondage to a strange god. Service to Egypt's god stands in the way of Yahweh's fulfillment of his promises, and so the conflict must be resolved. Deliverance of Israel from Pharaoh's power is a necessary prelude to the fulfillment of the promise of land.

THE PASSOVER LEGEND

It seems that the "bring out–bring in" combination at Deuteronomy 26 and elsewhere was basic to Israel's confession. Thus the

71

basic confession was brief, but to celebrate this wondrous event of Yahweh's deliverance of the slaves in Egypt, a festival was needed by the later community.

The nomadic rite used when shepherds move their flocks in the spring from desert to summer grazing grounds was a natural choice. It was connected with a passing over from one land to another, a fruitful land; it was a "bring out–bring in" event. The major elements of the festival can be gleaned from the earliest written record of the Passover regulations—that of the Yahwist at Exodus 12: 21–23.

1. Participation in the rite of the whole community (v. 21a)
2. Selection and sacrifice of an animal from the flock (v. 21b)
3. Smearing of doorposts (originally tent flaps) with the blood of the animal (v. 22)
4. Threat of "the destroyer" (v. 23)
5. Break up of the community in a hurry (see the act at vv. 33–34)

While no written record exists for such a nomadic festival (one could hardly expect it of ancient nomads), the elements from the J source outlined above, as well as the study of contemporary bedouins, seem to justify the arguments of scholars that such a rite had its home in the life of nomadic shepherds. The purpose of the rite was to protect the camp from a demon (called "the destroyer" at Exod. 12:23) as the people and their animals set out on their dangerous trek to find a new home.

The Priest's account of the Passover regulations at 12:1–20 is quite similar to the brief instructions of the Yahwist. The five elements of the old rite outlined above appear in the expanded Priestly form at verses 3–6, 7, 13, and 11. Here it becomes clear that the nomadic festival has been reinterpreted by Israel, for it is called "a passover to Yahweh" (v. 11).

The tradition which lies behind both J and P is that early Israel took over the nomadic rite for the annual departure from one pasture to another and historicized it to celebrate the once-and-for-all departure from the land of Egypt. Having taken over the old rite, the Israelites needed to explain some of the accompanying elements. Why sacrifice an animal? Why the blood on the doorposts? What will "the destroyer" do if there is no blood on the entrance? What does it all have to do with the departure from Egypt? In order to explain the details of the departure rite, the narrative about the slaughter of Egyptians took shape. The cultic celebration of the Passover gave impetus to the development of the narrative. Even the scope of the story seems to support this direction: the ritual description occupies thirty-four verses (P, 12:1–20, 43–49; J, 12: 21–27) but the event itself is recorded in two verses (12:39–40).

As the story is told, the firstborn of Egypt, even the Pharaoh's firstborn son, were smitten by the plague. This threat, present in the Priest's description of the rite (12:12) but not at all present in the Yahwist's, is yet a further development of the story in order to proclaim that in the midst of the salvation event Yahweh claimed Israel as his firstborn son (4:22–23). On the basis of the relationship of Israel as Yahweh's firstborn (cf. Jer. 31:9), the slaughter not of Egyptians in general but of Egypt's firstborn entered into the story.

This use of the Passover rite and the accompanying development of narrative led J. Pedersen to interpret all of Exodus 1—15 as a "Passover festival legend," regarding all the narrative material as an expansion from the nomadic rite (*Israel,* III–IV, pp. 384–415, 728– 737). Martin Noth accepts this interpretation for Exodus 1—13, but not for chapters 14—15. Perhaps it would be more correct to limit the scope to chapters 5—13. It is difficult, for example, to explain Exodus 1:8-14 as anything other than a historical reminiscence. Further, the Passover rite does not need a Moses, and so the traditions connecting the Yahweh name to the exodus through Moses in Exodus 3—4 could hardly have developed as part of the Passover legend.

THE PLAGUES

At Exodus 5:1 Moses and Aaron approached Pharaoh with Yahweh's demand that the people of Israel be set free in order to hold a feast in the wilderness. The king's response is classic: "Who is Yahweh, that I should obey him and send Israel out? I do not know Yahweh, and besides I will not send Israel out" (5:2). That was Pharaoh's mistake, for according to J, the plagues which follow serve the purpose of answering the king's question.

The plague stories which range from Exodus 7:8 through 10:29 are an interesting combination of the J and P sources. While some scholars find pieces of E scattered throughout the chapters, the source is not clearly discernible. As for the two sources which are present, J is attested at 7:14–18, 20b–21a, 23–24; 7:25—8:4; 8:8–15, 20–23; 9:1–7, 13–21, 23b–34; 10:1–11, 13b–19, 23–26, 28–29. P appears at 7:8–13, 19–20a, 21b–22; 8:5–7, 16–19; 9:8–12, 22–23a, 35; 10:12–13a, 20–22, 27.

Some of the issues which arise out of this delineation of sources are the following: (1) the roles of Moses and Aaron, (2) the nature of the plagues, (3) the purposes of the plagues, (4) the hardness of heart motif.

(1) In the J material Moses alone plays a role, although the one who brings the plagues is Yahweh himself. Even when Aaron is mentioned alongside Moses, he is not involved in the action. The nature of Moses' role is that of mediator in the drama. His function is to announce what Yahweh will do if Pharaoh stubbornly refuses to let the people go. Even in the story of the Nile's water becoming blood, it is not clear if Yahweh or Moses strikes the water with the rod (see 7:17).

In P, by contrast, Aaron is the active figure. He performs tricks involving a metamorphosis: rod becomes serpent, water becomes blood, dust becomes gnats; only in the case of the frogs is there no such transformation. In all cases the plague is effected by the use of Aaron's rod, and so there is a more magical quality here. In the latter plagues Moses becomes the actor and once accomplishes a metamorphosis: ashes become boils. For the most part the references to Moses are extremely brief and often are considered to be redactional pieces.

(2) The plagues are often explained by natural means. What is striking in the story, however, is the uniqueness of the events at the hand of Yahweh. Further, in several of the plagues, the Hebrew storyteller seems to be emphasizing that natural phenomena near and dear to the Egyptians were turned against them by the power of Yahweh. The Nile River was in every sense the life-giving force to Egypt; with Yahweh at work for his people, the Nile became abhorrent. Frogs were associated with the annual flooding of the Nile which brought rich soil and needed water for agriculture; now because of Pharaoh's refusal to let the people go, the frogs appeared in such abundance that they became despicable to Egypt. The

plague of darkness surely must have been directed at Egypt's fascination with and worship of the sun, for in Egyptian mythology the sun god Re battled the dragon Apophis every night; darkness for three days indicated the sun god was being defeated.

Related to that twist of things Egyptian recorded in both sources is the Priest's contest between Aaron's magic rod and the magicians of Egypt. In the first round, after Aaron changed the rod into a snake, the Egyptians did the same, but Aaron's rod swallowed up the others. That humorous scene almost seems to set the stage for the next two rounds. When the magicians duplicated the transformation of the water into blood and the multiplication of frogs, they simply made matters worse! Finally their defeat is described progressively as they first were unable to duplicate the gnats plague and then as they themselves were covered with boils.

(3) The Yahwist is emphatic about the purpose of the plagues as an answer to the Pharaoh's question: Who is Yahweh? "In order that you may know that I am Yahweh" occurs in various forms several times as the purpose for sending a plague (7:17; 8:22; 9:14, 16) and for its removal (8:10; 9:29). The reference at 10:1–2 seems to argue that the purpose for all the plagues is that Moses and Israel, not Pharaoh, will know "I am Yahweh" and thus appears to belong to a different author.

The purpose of the Priest's plagues is not so explicit. The closest that writer comes is 11:9: "that my wonders may be multiplied in the land of Egypt."

(4) The hardness of heart motif raises the question "Why would God deliberately make someone stubborn in order to bring plagues?" The source delineation above shows that the expressions regarding the motif vary. The Yahwist uses two expressions: "the heart of Pharaoh was hardened" (*kbd*; 7:14; 9:7), and "Pharaoh hardened his heart" (*kbd;* 8:15, 32; 9:34). In no case does the Yahwist attribute the hardening act to Yahweh. The purpose of the expression is to show that the plagues do not produce results.

Likewise the Priest has two expressions: "Pharaoh's heart was hardened" (*ḥzq*; 7:13, 22; 8:19) and "Yahweh hardened Pharaoh's heart" (*ḥzq;* 9:12; 10:20, 27). Once, in introducing to Moses the divine plan, Yahweh himself said, "I will harden (*qšh*) Pharaoh's heart" (7:3). Thus the Priest seems to set up the expressions in the plague narratives with a sequence in mind: first, in a passive sense, Pharaoh's heart was hardened; second, in an active sense, Yahweh caused it to happen. The point is that just as Pharaoh first chose to make himself stubborn, Yahweh later chose it for him. The purpose here is to introduce the reason for each plague. Eventually some great act of judgment will be necessary for Israel's deliverance (7:3–4). This final act will be the deliverance at the sea (compare 7:5 with 14:18).

In conclusion, the plagues from 7:14—10:29 result in nothing but Pharaoh's stubbornness and Israel's continued slavery. The stories present in dramatic fashion every attempt by Yahweh through Moses and Aaron to deliver the people from their oppression. Every attempt but one: Yahweh has not yet caused the death of a single Egyptian. In order to justify that final act of slaughtering Egypt's firstborn, the plague stories grew up and were written down by our two major sources. Without allowing ambiguity (so Robertson) the plagues lead to no sympathy for the villain at the final blow. These plagues can be understood only in light of the Passover legend and belong to its development.

THE EVENT AT THE SEA

There is another climax to the exodus event besides the Passover legend. It is the event at the sea which is attested in the immediate context by three traditions: J, P, and the Song of Moses. In order to include this second climax in the story, it is necessary that Pharaoh change his mind about the release and pursue the people with his cavalry (14:5–9). Thus the stage was set for another drama in the continuing conflict between Yahweh, the God of Israel, and Pharaoh, god of Egypt.

The sources J and P can be separated nicely into two complete accounts presently intertwined at Exodus 14:10–31.

"J"

v. 10 . . . the people of Israel lifted up their eyes, and behold, the Egyptians were marching after them; and they were in great fear. vv. 13–14 And Moses said to the people, "Fear not, stand firm and see the salvation of the Lord, which he will work for you today; for the Egyptians whom you see today, you shall never see again. The Lord will fight for you, and you have only to be still."

vv. 19–20 . . . and the pillar of cloud moved from before them and stood behind them, coming between the host of Egypt and the host of Israel. And there was the cloud and the darkness; and the night passed without one coming near the other all night.

v. 21 . . . and the Lord drove the sea back by a strong east wind all night, and made the sea dry land . . .
v. 24 And in the morning watch the Lord in the pillar of fire and of cloud looked down upon the host of the Egyptians, and discomfited the host of the Egyptians,
v. 25 clogging their chariot wheels so that they drove heavily; and the Egyptians said, "Let us flee from before Israel; for the Lord fights for them against the Egyptians."

v. 27 . . . and the sea returned to its wonted flow when the morning appeared; and the Egyptians fled into it, and the Lord routed (actually "shook off") the Egyptians in the midst of the sea.

vv. 30–31 Thus the Lord saved Israel that day from the hand of the Egyptians; and Israel saw the Egyptians dead upon the seashore. And Israel saw the great work which the Lord did against the Egyptians, and the people feared the Lord; and they believed in the Lord and in his servant Moses.

The basic structure of the Yahwist's account is built upon stereotyped formulas from Holy War traditions, those battles in which Yahweh fights for Israel against the foe. After recording the advance of the Egyptians and the resulting fear of the people Israel, the Yahwist portrays Moses as a speaker who says "Fear not, stand firm and see the victory of Yahweh, which he will work for you today; . . . The Lord will fight for you. . . ." The initial words "fear not" occur in the face of enemy threat elsewhere. Moreover, the following imperatives "stand firm and see the victory of the Lord" are paralleled almost precisely at 2 Chronicles 20:17 where likewise it follows a "fear not" (v. 15).

The command to be silent (*ḥrs* "to be still," *RSV*) occurs frequently but not in connection with war scenes. However, a parallel word (*rph*) occurs in the context of a battle against Jerusalem at Psalm 46:11 ("Be still"). The expression "Yahweh will fight for you" occurs frequently in battle stories. Particularly interesting is Yahweh's act of "discomfiting" (*RSV*) the Egyptians; the term has to do with a panic (*hûm*) in which the enemy accomplishes its own destruction. That the enemy "flees" (*nûs*) is attested often in Holy

War stories. Finally, the element of "seeing" the victory seems to belong to such war traditions.

Thus, while these terms appear in a wide variety of texts, all the passages deal with battles in which Yahweh is the victorious warrior. For clusters of these expressions in the same passages see Exodus 23:23–33; Deuteronomy 7:17–26; Joshua 10:6–14; Judges 4:12–16; 1 Samuel 7:5–11; 2 Chronicles 20:13–23; Psalms 46, 48. (The classic work on the Holy War tradition is that of von Rad, *Der Heilige Krieg*; see also Cross, "Divine Warrior in Israel's Early Cult," *Biblical Motifs,* pp. 11–30.)

In addition to the stereotyped formulas, each narrative containing these elements has its own characteristics relating to the enemy, the place, and specific acts of Yahweh, especially his weapons of war. At Joshua 10:6–11 "Yahweh threw down great stones from heaven." "Hornets" are his weapon in Exodus 23:28 and Deuteronomy 7:20. In the Yahwist's sea event of Exodus 14 Yahweh uses an "east wind" and "the sea" (vv. 21, 27). Both are loaded with mythological overtones. The "east wind" appears frequently in the Old Testament to effect Yahweh's judgment (cf. Ps. 45:7; Ezek. 27:26; Job 27:21; Jer. 4:11; 18:17; Isa. 27:8; Hos. 13:15; Exod. 10:13). Outside of the Old Testament, "wind" appears as the instrument which Marduk used in order to defeat Tiamat, the monster of chaos, the symbol of evil (*Enuma elish* IV 45, 96, 98; see *ANET,* pp. 66f.); that wind is called *imḫullu,* the evil wind often associated with the onslaught of disease in Mesopotamian literature.

The "sea" (Heb. *yam*) brings to mind that mythology of Mesopotamia and Canaan in which the sea is the adversary of the god of order and fertility. In the Ugaritic texts the foe of Baal is indeed named Yamm ("sea"). As an adversary of Yahweh, Yamm appears in the Old Testament at Nahum 1:4 and Habakkuk 3:8–9. The mythological concept of making dry the sea (v. 21) seems to play an important role in the Yahwist's narrative. At Exodus 14, however, it is Pharaoh and not Yamm who is Yahweh's opponent. Thus, the sea becomes an instrument of the Lord's deliverance rather than the object of his indignation.

Unusual in this battle story is the emphasis by the Yahwist on darkness. In no other description of the sea event and in none of the Holy War passages cited above does the battle occur in the night.

Here in Exodus 14, however, the emphasis on the night is striking: so dark that one cannot see another (v. 20); the morning watch occurs when the sky is yet dark, and so the pillar consists of fire as well as cloud (v. 24); finally the enemy is defeated "toward morning" (v. 27), and later Israel was able to see the effect: Egyptians dead on the seashore (v. 30).

That climactic reference to time "toward morning" (*RSV* "when [the] morning appeared") raises the probability of more mythological allusion. The precise expression *lipnôt bōqer* occurs also at Psalm 46:5 (Heb. v. 6); the context is a battle in which Yahweh protected Jerusalem from enemy attack. His presence in the city assures the inhabitants that God will help her "toward morning" (*RSV* "right early"). Following the victory the people are invited to see what Yahweh had done in battle (vv. 8–9), and then occurs the familiar "Be still" (v. 10). The expression occurs also in the story of the rape of the Levite's concubine at Gibeah. The "base fellows" of the city abused her all night, and then "toward morning" (*RSV* "as morning appeared") the woman fell down dead at the door of the house where her master found her in the morning (Judg. 19:25–27). Finally a similar expression occurs at Isaiah 17:14. The little sermon in verses 12–14 speaks of a raging battle (apparently against Jerusalem) in which Yahweh will rebuke the enemy and they will "flee far away." The climax occurs in the final verse with the words:

> At evening time, behold, terror!
> Before morning (*bᵉterem bōqer*), they are no more!
> This is the portion of those who despoil us,
>   and the lot of those who plunder us.

Thus the three cases of *lipnôt bōqer* and the one comparable expression *bᵉterem bōqer* speak of (1) a conflict which occurs during the night, and (2) a resolution of the conflict "toward/before morning." Moreover, in all cases except Isaiah 17:12–14 appears another element: (3) third party observation of the resolution (see also, without the "toward morning" expression, 2 Kings 19:35–36).

While it is difficult to date and locate the origins of the Gibeah outrage in Judges 19, the location of the other three texts is clear: Jerusalem. Psalm 46 is a song about "the city of God" where Yahweh Sabaoth is present. Isaiah the prophet preached in Jerusalem exclusively. And the Yahwist himself did his work, it seems, in the Davidic-Solomonic court. There is no evidence to conclude that the other three writers had in mind the Yahwist's sea event and borrowed the imagery from the exodus. Rather it seems that all these Holy War traditions of Jerusalem had a peculiar twist: the battle occurred at night and was resolved "toward morning." These traditions of war were probably connected with the theme of the invincibility of Jerusalem attested in Psalms 46, 48, 76, and frequently in the preaching of Isaiah (see von Rad, *Old Testament Theology*, *II*, pp. 155–169). That the mythological imagery surrounds such a theme can be seen in the description of the enemy in terms of roaring waters, raging nations, kings assembled, and thundering sea.

In ancient Near Eastern texts one can find in the Egyptian myth of the sun god a parallel to this threefold scheme of nocturnal conflict, resolution "toward morning," and third party observation in the morning. The god Re enters the western horizon every evening where during the night he battles Apophis, the dragon of the deep. The appearance of morning on the eastern horizon signals the victory of the sun god.

One can only ask if the Yahwist had in mind this common Egyptian myth when he incorporated into his Holy War scheme the night-morning outline. If so, his story becomes a powerful and dynamic account of how Yahweh—not Re or Pharaoh or the Egyptians—was victorious after his nocturnal combat in the sea—and against the Egyptians, no less! Thus, it might be that this peculiar slant to the Holy War battle appears here precisely because the enemy was Egypt. On the other hand, the "toward morning" motif might simply have been integral to the Jerusalem form of Holy War traditions and thus used here—quite coincidentally—in the battle against the Egyptians.

In any case, the Yahwist described the exodus event in terms of Holy War imagery with a Jerusalem twist. Thus, in spite of the apparent naturalness of the story—wind drying a marshy area where the Egyptians became stuck in the mud—the story is highly mythological in expression, stereotyped in style, and miraculous in portrayal. Everything is used in his presentation to make the point we have seen consistently in the Yahwist's source: the action of deliverance is exclusively that of Yahweh; "You have only to be still."

The result of his action is the people's belief in Yahweh and in Moses.

The Priest makes the miraculous even more pronounced. As in the plague stories, the Priestly writer makes use of the rod which, when stretched out over the sea, divided it so that the sea became two walls of water for the Israelites to pass through. Safe on the opposite shore, Moses was instructed to stretch out the rod again, and the walls came tumbling down on the Egyptians, drowning every last one of them. This particular imagery of dividing the waters is attested elsewhere in describing the sea event (Ps. 78:13; Isa. 63:12; Neh. 9:11).

The spectacular image of the two walls of waters is impressive to the imagination. Aarre Lauha has shown that the renewed (or new) interest in the sea event during the exilic period (cf. Isa. 50:2; especially 51:9–10; 43:16–17), and particularly the miraculous description of the event, came about because of the creation conflict story of Marduk and Tiamat in Babylon. In order to demonstrate the mighty power of Yahweh in the midst of these cosmic deities and their battle, the witnesses of the exilic period enhanced the spectacular element of the exodus (*VT Supplement* [1963], 32–46).

The Priest had other issues to settle here too. According to that writer, when God revealed his name Yahweh to Moses and commissioned Moses and Aaron to serve as spokesmen to Pharaoh, the Lord said that he would harden Pharaoh's heart and bring without result signs and wonders. Then "I will lay my hand upon Egypt and bring forth my hosts . . . out of the land of Egypt by great acts of judgment. And the Egyptians shall know that I am Yahweh . . ." (Exod. 7:4–5). Now the time had arrived. As Pharaoh's army drew near, Yahweh explained to Moses that he "will harden the hearts of the Egyptians" as he did earlier to Pharaoh in order to effect the plagues (9:12; 10:20, 27; cf. 7:13, 22; 8:19; 9:35). This time, however, the issue will be settled: "I will get glory over Pharaoh and all his host, . . . And the Egyptians shall know that I am Yahweh . . . (14:17–18).

Only here in connection with the act of deliverance does the Priest use the "know that I am Yahweh" formula which occurred so frequently in the Yahwist's story of the plagues. In this respect the Priestly writer of the sixth century B.C. sounds again so much like

Ezekiel, who more than seventy times looks forward to the return from exile as the moment when you/they shall know that I am Yahweh. Thus the Priest's audience and situation seem to have affected his account of the sea event in substantial ways: as Yahweh was overwhelmingly powerful against the ruler of Egypt, he is and will be powerful over the might of Babylon; when that victory occurs, the nations will know that he is Yahweh.

Finally, a third witness to the deliverance at the sea is incorporated into the context: the Song of Moses in Exodus 15:1-18. This song has been and continues to be one of the most debated passages in the Old Testament. The stylistic features of the poem have led some to conclude it is ancient (see especially the work of Cross and Freedman, *JNES*, 1955). Others, especially Martin Noth (*Exodus*, pp. 123-126), on the basis of tradition-criticism argue that the song is relatively late. Whatever its date of origin, study of the song strikes the reader as simultaneously full of mythological imagery and yet quite concerned about the specificity of geography and history. In its total structure the poem consists of two parts which reflect the common "bring out–bring in" sequence we have observed in the little historical confessions: verses 1-12 describe the victory of Yahweh over Pharaoh's army at the Reed Sea (not specifically an exodus), while verses 13-18 tell of the victory of Yahweh over the inhabitants of Canaan and the settlement of the people in the land.

The hymn witnesses to Yahweh's leading and guiding his redeemed to his "holy abode" (Heb. *nᵉwēh qodšekā*) which, after mention of the terror of the Canaanites at hearing Yahweh's deed, is further defined.

> You will bring them in,
>> and plant them on the mount of your possession (*bᵉhar naḥᵃlatᵉkā*),
> the place (*mākôn*), Yahweh, which you have made for your abode (*lᵉšibtᵉkā*),
> the sanctuary, (*miqqᵉdaš*), O Lord, which your
> hands have established.
> Yahweh will be king for ever and ever (15:17-18; author's translation).

An Ugaritic text from the latter half of the second millenium B.C. describes the sanctuary of Baal in strikingly similar terms. That god invites sister Anath to visit him where he will reveal to her a secret "in the midst of my mount godly Zaphon," described as "the sanctuary" (*bqdš*), "mount of my possession" (*bǵr nḥlty*).

On the basis of this parallel, some scholars have interpreted the passage in Exodus 15 to mean Mt. Zion where Yahweh's sanctuary stood. Such an identification would date the song sometime after Solomon's temple was built. The use of *naḥ⁽a⁾lâ* for the Jerusalem temple at Psalm 79:1 and Jeremiah 12:7 would support such a view. On the other hand, *naḥ⁽a⁾lâ* is used much more frequently in the Old Testament to refer to the land of Canaan which Yahweh gave to Israel (e.g., Deut. 4:21; 15:4; Jer. 12:14). Moreover, Psalm 78 speaks of the land of Ephraim as "the territory of his holiness" in synonymous parallelism with "the mountain which his right hand won" (v. 54) and as "a portion of inheritance" (v. 55). The context of Exodus 15:13–18 itself seems to point to the land of Canaan rather than Jerusalem per se. As for Yahweh's kingship, it is not necessary to assume a Jerusalem location or an established Israelite monarchy as the basis for such a confession. Thus, the "bring in" at the beginning of verse 17 probably refers to the land, as it does so frequently in the "bring out–bring in" passages we have discussed previously.

The insertion of the hymn into the present context serves two functions: (1) it demonstrates that the people's response to Yahweh's deliverance is joyful praise and confession (like Judg. 4—5); and (2) it brings to a conclusion the exodus event with the acclamation that Yahweh is king. Just as the Babylonian Marduk became king after his victory over Tiamat, just as Baal became king following his victory over Yamm, so Yahweh becomes king on the basis of his victory—mythologically described—over the historical Pharaoh of Egypt. This theme of victory followed by acclamation of kingship is a powerful one in the Old Testament, as can be seen elsewhere at Isaiah 52:7–10; 24:21–23; Psalms 47, 93, 96, 98, 99.

In conclusion, there are two basic "bring out" traditions: Passover and the sea event. The J and P sources attest to both of these traditions, and the Song of Moses is a third witness to the latter tradition. All of these witnesses to both traditions are maintained within five chapters of biblical material, Exodus 11—15. Some relief to this congestion has been suggested by George W. Coats who argues that the motifs in the sea event connect it to the wilderness tradition rather than the exodus which has already occurred in the Passover event (see *VT* 22 [1972] 288–295). Those arguments are more pertinent to J than to P, but even in J the theme of the battle against Pharaoh seems to look backward as far as Exodus 1 as well as forward. It seems to the present writer that the Yahwistic record of the sea is presented in such a way that it serves as a transition between the exodus and wilderness traditions. Motifs important to both are brought together to climax the battle as well as to begin the leading motif.

The cluster of traditions about the departure from Egypt serves to demonstrate how important this exodus confession was for the people of Israel. The belief that "Yahweh brought us out" took many different dramatic forms. In some cases, neither Passover nor sea is mentioned (Exod. 20:2; Deut. 6:21–23; 26:5–9; 1 Sam. 12:8; Hos. 11:1; 12:13; Amos 9:7). In other cases, the Passover event is attested but not the sea (Pss. 105:36–37; 135:8–9). As for the sea itself, sometimes it is dried up (J in Exod. 14; Isa. 50:2; 51:10); occasionally it is divided (P in Exod. 14; Pss. 78:12–13; 136:10–15; cf. Isa. 43:16–17); in one case it overflows (Deut. 11: 2–4); it is called the Reed Sea only rarely (Exod. 15:4; Deut. 11:2– 4; Josh. 24:6; Pss. 106:9; 136:13, 15). As for the human agents, Moses clearly plays an important role in P but not in J where he simply recites the Holy War formula; in Exodus 15 Moses plays no role at all. In fact, only rarely do Moses and Aaron appear in the recitation of the tradition (Josh. 24:5; 1 Sam. 12:8; Pss. 77:20; 105:26; cf. Hos. 12:13).

All this diversity leads to the conclusion that we cannot reconstruct what happened when the people who later became Israel escaped from Egypt. There is sufficient historical evidence to demonstrate that Semites were living in Egypt in the "Goshen" area in the latter half of the second millenium B.C. Moreover, there is overwhelming traditional evidence that people who came out of Egypt became members of Israel. However, that "Yahweh brought us out" is strictly a matter of faith; it is a confession based upon the revelation of God that his hand is at work in the events of history. Ultimately, in the form of the miracle at the sea, the exodus confession became a paradigm for eschatological salvation (see Isa. 43:19ff; 51:9ff.).

CHAPTER SEVEN

THE TIME BETWEEN

Immediately after Miriam's victory song at the sea (Exod. 15:21), Moses led Israel "into the wilderness of Shur," and with that movement began the forty-year period of insecurity in the desert. The traditions about this experience serve, on the one hand, as a transition from exodus to Sinai (Exod. 15:22—18:27) and, on the other hand, as a link between Mt. Sinai and the entrance into the Promised Land (Num. 11:33—36:13). That division around Sinai material is neither a mere literary nor geographical construction; it is a theological issue which divides the wilderness experience into these two sections: apostasy.

The wilderness traditions, however, seem to be more closely related to exodus than to Sinai. Wilderness is not mentioned in the little historical confessions at Deuteronomy 6:21-23; 26:5-9; 1 Samuel 12:8, or in the larger hymnic recital of history in Psalm 135. In all those texts the "bring out–bring in" pattern excludes any intervening traditions. However, in the historical summary at Joshua 24:7 and 17, between the exodus and the entrance into the land, are brief allusions to the wilderness. Wilderness occupies that same position between exodus and land in the psalmic recitals of history at Psalms 105:39-41; 106:13-15, 28-32; 78:17-41, 52-53; 136: 16, and also at Amos 2:10.

In the Old Testament as a whole, and in the Tetrateuch in particular, the wilderness time was interpreted both positively and negatively. On the one hand, it was a time when the Lord and the people were on intimate terms; on the other hand, the wilderness period was the scene of utter rebellion on the part of Israel.

THE TIME OF GOD'S CARE

The view that looked back to the wilderness as the time of intimacy between Yahweh and Israel is attested in a variety of texts. In these texts the verbs used for the action of Yahweh indicate the positive nature of the experience: "preserved" (Josh. 24:17), "led" (Deut. 8:2, 15; 29:5; Ps. 136:16; Amos 2:10), "brought . . . gave . . . remembered" (Ps. 105:40–42), "found" (Hos. 9:10), "knew" (Hos. 13:5; Deut. 2:7). These terms stress the care which Yahweh provided for the people in the dangerous trek through the wilderness. He supplied their every need—physical and spiritual—at a time and in a place at which they were helpless and on their own. Although in some cases Israel "asked" for sustenance, the action was exclusively God's as he moved the people between Egypt and his Promised Land.

Among northern circles in particular, this time of intimacy is explicated further. Hosea portrays the wilderness as the golden age to which Israel must return in order to reestablish the marriage bond that existed before Israel's adultery with Canaanite baals. That Yahweh would "seduce" her into the wilderness and speak "to her heart" would provide Israel opportunity to respond faithfully "as in the days of her youth and at the time she came up from the land of Egypt" (Hos. 2:14–15 [Heb. 16–17]). The same sexual image seems to lie behind another text in Hosea where Yahweh says, "It was I who knew you in the wilderness" (13:5; see Gen. 4:1). Yet it is the word at Hosea 9:10 which supports the thesis of R. Bach that a special "finding tradition" explained Israel's election in the wilderness where Yahweh discovered her: "Like grapes in the wilderness I found Israel. . . ."

Likewise Jeremiah, trained in northern traditions (Jer. 1:1), looked back longingly on the wilderness period as one of intimacy.

Thus says the Lord,
I remember the devotion of your youth,
  your love as a bride,
how you followed me in the wilderness,
  in a land not sown.
Israel was holy to the Lord,
  the first fruits of his harvest (Jer. 2:2–3).

As soon as Israel entered Canaan and enjoyed its fruits and good things, she exchanged gods: Baal for Yahweh (2:4–13). The time of intimacy came to an adulterous end.

In Deuteronomy, where northern traditions seem to prevail, the imagery is changed somewhat, and a new interpretation is placed on the wilderness. The intimate relationship is not one of husband and wife but of father and son. Like a good wisdom teacher (see Prov. 3:11–12) the author of Deuteronomy 8 put together two short homilies (vv. 1–10 and vv. 11–18 respectively) in order to emphasize that the wilderness experience was one in which Yahweh humbled, tested, and disciplined Israel "as a man disciplines his son" (v. 5). More explicitly, this guidance "through the great and terrible wilderness" with all its trials had as its purpose "that he might humble you and test you, to do you good in the end" (vv. 15–16). This new interpretation is radicalized when the writer contrasts manna with food in order to teach Israel a new lesson: the only source of life is the word of the Lord (v. 3).

This understanding of the wilderness as the favorable time in which God cared for his people is attested in the narratives of Exodus and Numbers. This is particularly true in those stories which are structured along the lines which Brevard Childs labels Pattern I (*Book of Exodus,* pp. 258ff.), the elements of which are (a) an initial need, (b) a complaint, (c) an intercession by Moses, (d) God's miraculous intervention to meet the need.

These elements of Pattern I appear most clearly in Exodus 15:22–25; 17:1–7; Numbers 20:1–13. (a) All three stories express the legitimate need for water in the wilderness—at Marah, Rephidim, and Kadesh respectively. (b) On the basis of this need the people "murmured" (*lûn*) or "contended" (*rîb*) against Moses, in the latter two cases complaining specifically that he had brought them out of Egypt. (c) In the Exodus passages Moses "cried to the Lord" (both J), but in Numbers 20 (P) Moses' intercession took the form of joining Aaron at the door of the tent of meeting in a posture of silent humility and adoration ("on their faces," v. 6). (d) In each case God instructed Moses in the use of some particular instrument in order to provide the needed water for the people: in Exodus 15:25 a tree thrown into the water made the bitter water sweet and drinkable; at Exodus 17:5–6 and at Numbers 20:8ff. the old familiar rod was used for striking a rock out of which gushed water. (The Yahwist refers specifically to the rod with which Moses struck the Nile [cf. 7:17] and thus pulls together tightly the exodus and the

wilderness traditions.) Thus Yahweh cared for the people's legitimate need in the wilderness, just as the Old Testament traditions
elsewhere attested. Yet in all three stories the subsequent response
of the people is missing.

The account of the gift of manna at Exodus 16 has a different
structure, but attests nevertheless to God's care. The account is a
combination of the two sources J and P, each of which has its own
particular emphasis. J material seems to include verses 4–5 which
relate the promise of God that he would rain bread from heaven for
the people to eat each day; the purpose is clearly stated: that I may
test them (v. 4). On the sixth day the amount to be brought in will
be double that of the previous five days. Apparently the daily gift was
granted and the people gathered accordingly. But then, J continues
at verses 27–31 to describe the Lord's anger that the greedy people
went out to gather on the seventh day, the sabbath. In a sense, the
Lord's test was downright unfair, because thus far in the Bible there
has been given no law regarding the sabbath. What commandment
or law did the people break? As it turns out, it seems that the whole
episode was nothing more than a pedagogical device to teach the
people the meaning of the sabbath and to provide for its observance.
Thus, according to J, the sabbath day of rest for the people was
established in the wilderness.

Apart from those seven verses from J, the entire chapter is from
P. This account relates the murmuring of the people against Moses
and Aaron because of hunger (the need is not explicated first, as in
Pattern I). They contrasted the wilderness, into which the two leaders brought them, with Egypt where food was abundant. Moses (and
Aaron) responded to the complaint by saying that at evening time,
when meat would be available, the people would know that it was
not they, the leaders, but Yahweh who brought them out of Egypt
and into the wilderness. Moreover, in the morning the people themselves would see the glory of the Lord, accompanied by the gift of
bread. As it turned out, the people saw the Lord's glory almost immediately; it served the function of divine address through Moses
that the people would indeed have meat in the evening and bread in
the morning. "Then you shall know that I am Yahweh your God"—
that well-known self-identification formula so common in J's plague
stories and so unique in P's sea event (14:18). In the plagues and

at the sea, it was Pharaoh and his fellow Egyptians who came to know that he was Yahweh. Now, in the wilderness, by the gracious care of the Lord for his people's physical need of hunger, Israel herself will come to know who he is!

As the account from P continues, the meat gift, packaged as quails, is hardly mentioned (v. 13a) while all the emphasis is placed on the manna. Moses instructed the amazed people to collect an omer for each person in the tent. Miraculously, no matter how much or how little the collector put in the shopping cart, it turned out to be an omer. Everyone's need was cared for by the assigned portion for each day. Nothing was to be hoarded for the following day; when some tried to do just that, the manna became wormy and foul. According to von Rad, the powerful lesson from the story is that "this daily sustenance by God demanded a surrender without security: in dealing with God, we live from minute to minute" (*Old Testament Theology,* I, p. 282). It was only on the sixth day that the people were allowed to gather two omers apiece, because "tomorrow is a day of solemn rest, a holy sabbath to the Lord . . ." (v. 23). This time, no food spoiled. No bread was given, and none collected on the sabbath day. Thus in startling fashion, the rest which God appropriated for himself at creation (Gen. 2:1–3), he now gave to his people that they might also appropriate it and build their lives upon it.

This relationship of God's rest to the people's rest begins a new biblical theme. Rest takes the form of God's presence with his people (Exod. 33:14), particularly on the Ark in the Jerusalem temple (1 Chron. 23:25; Ps. 138:8, 14; but cf. Isa. 66:1). The land itself is an expression of God's gift of rest (e.g., Num. 10:33; Deut. 3:20), as is also security from enemies in that land (e.g., Deut. 12:10; 2 Sam. 7:1). Understandably, rest became an eschatalogical hope (Isa. 11:10; 32:18). Since the theme was addressed to the hardships of human life and to humanity's relationship to God in the present and in the future, rest was reinterpreted in the New Testament as having been fulfilled in Christ. By faith Christians can enter into God's creation rest, as Israelites could do in the wilderness (Heb. 3:7—4:13; see von Rad, *Problems in the Hexateuch,* pp. 94ff.).

By placing J's promise of food immediately after the Priest's account of murmuring, the redactor highlighted the origin of "bread."

The complaint: "Would that we had died by the hand of the Lord in the land of Egypt, when we sat by the fleshpots and ate bread to the full; . . ." (v. 3, P).

The response: "Then the Lord said to Moses, 'Behold, I will rain bread from heaven for you; . . .' " (v. 4, J).

While the people longed for the security of food they had in Egypt, Yahweh announced that their source of food and life itself was in his hands, even in the wilderness.

The food itself fits the description of a natural substance in the Sinai peninsula. Modern investigators have discovered that insects puncture the fruit of the tamarisk trees to excrete a certain substance. This sap forms a congealed pellet during the cool evening hours and melts in the warmth of the sun. As pellets the sap can be cooked to make a sort of bread. Thus the story of the manna reflects the somewhat common experience of inhabitants in the wilderness. But in the narratives of Exodus 16 that natural substance is interpreted to be the gift from heaven by which the Lord provided food for his people's need and which led to the establishment of the sabbath as a day of human, as well as divine, rest.

Equally surprising as the institution of the sabbath rest in the wilderness is the establishment of the system for administering justice. In Exodus 18 the Elohist records that Moses' father-in-law, the priest of Midian, came to the wilderness of Sinai to meet Moses and the motley crew who came with him out of Egypt. Quite astonishingly, this Midianite priest announced that he was convinced there was no god greater than Yahweh (v. 11). Then, as though he were a priest of Yahweh (perhaps he was!), Jethro offered sacrifices to God while Aaron joined the elders in the congregation. The next day, Jethro discovered that Moses was overworked by having to deal with all the disputes among the people. And so, in the manner of a wisdom teacher, the old priest admonished his son-in-law to heed, offered him counsel, urged Moses to teach "the way," and then to select men who "fear God," are trustworthy, and hate a bribe (vv. 19–21). These qualified men would serve as judges for the minor disputes, thus freeing Moses himself to concentrate on the hard cases.

The chapter has been the subject of much scholarly discussion, primarily because of the role the priest of Midian played in the cult of Yahweh and in the legal system of Israel. In light of the hatred for Midianites during the period of the judges and in the early monarchy, this tradition regarding the relationship of Moses and the Midianites seems to reach back to an early time. Whether Yahweh was originally a Midianite god who came to be Israel's through some means akin to the "Kenite hypothesis" is not our concern here. Our interest is in this one more example of the Lord's care for the people in the wilderness. In this time he fed the people and gave them water to drink; he protected them from enemy attack. Beyond that he also cared for justice among the people as they lived between Egypt and the Promised Land.

At the same time Yahweh demonstrated care for Moses as he used the Midianite to organize a better system to relieve his servant of an overbearing burden. Not even his commissioned persons are asked to work the impossible. The promise given at the call itself "I am with you" (Exod. 3:12) here took the form of needed relief.

THE TIME OF THE PEOPLE'S REBELLION

The anger of Moses at the people's hoarding of manna (16:20) and the anger of Yahweh at their greed (16:28) leads to consideration of the more prevalent attitude toward the wilderness: it was a time of rebellion and of testing the Lord. Already in 15:24 and 17:3 the people murmured against Moses—but for good reason: they were thirsty. Less commendable is their murmuring at 16:2 where their complaining against Moses and Aaron did not follow such a specified need. But when the people left Mt. Sinai to resume their wilderness experience, as the Book of Numbers reports, the murmuring was more serious, and so was the Lord's response.

The narratives of Numbers introduce us to what Brevard Childs calls Pattern II (*Book of Exodus,* pp. 258ff.). The elements of this pattern are as follows: (a) an initial complaint, (b) God's anger and punishment, (c) intercession from Moses, (d) a reprieve of the punishment.

These features are most clearly seen at Numbers 11:1–3; 16:41–50 (Heb. 17:6–15); 21:4–10. (a) The complaining which began immediately after the people set foot from Mt. Sinai concerned general misfortune (11:1). After Korah's rebellion in chapter 16, the people murmured against Moses and Aaron because the rebels were killed

(16:41). Later, when the people became impatient with the journey itself, they spoke against God and Moses about lack of water and food (21:4–5). These complaints are a far cry from the earlier stated necessity of water in Pattern I. (b) The angry response of the Lord took the form of a consuming fire, a deadly plague, and a serpent attack. (c) Moses intercession consisted of prayer, and somewhat more magically, a racing priest (Aaron) with burning incense in his censer, and a bronze serpent on a pole. (d) In all cases the fatalities ceased immediately. All this action is totally different from the stories in Pattern I and from Exodus 16.

Throughout Numbers 11—21, the motif of murmuring is consistent, and the Lord's response is anything but cordial. In 11:4–13, 18–23, 31–35 is the record of the people's complaint about the non-protein nature of their diet (recall Exod. 16:3). They had had enough of that manna; they desired the variety they enjoyed in Egypt, particularly meat. Yahweh promised to give them a month's full of meat—until it became disgusting to them. As it turned out, the Lord sent quails in abundance. But while the people were still chewing the first morsels of the meat, the Lord sent a plague which killed a multitude. The burials were so many that the place was called "graves of craving" (11:34).

As we have seen above, Numbers 20:1–13 is structured along the lines of Pattern I, for the need for water was a legitimate complaint. The story concludes, however, on a down beat compared to the other spring stories at Exodus 15:22–25 and 17:1–7. Here the Lord announced to Moses and Aaron that because they "did not believe in me, to sanctify me in the eyes of the people of Israel," they would not enter the Promised Land (see also Deut. 32:50–52 in contrast to the vicarious suffering of Moses at Deut. 4:21–22). This Priestly motive for Moses' and Aaron's failure to enter the land is based apparently on the failure of the two leaders to heed the Lord's instructions: though they were commanded to "tell the rock . . . to yield its water" (20:7), nevertheless they struck it with the rod (20:11, see J's record at Exod. 17:1–7). This was interpreted as failure to sanctify (qdš) Yahweh at Meribah-Kadesh (Deut. 32:51).

The reason for murmuring in Numbers 13—14 is fear of enemies. When the spies sent to Canaan returned with the report that the Canaanites were giants who devour people, the Israelites murmured against Moses and Aaron that they would have been better off staying in Egypt. In fact, they proposed to return. Yahweh threatened them with pestilence, but Moses interceded with the question, "What will the neighbors think if you aren't able to get these people to the land?" The Lord was persuaded by the argument but made clear that none of the people who tested him these ten times would enter the land (14:20–23).

Throughout the wilderness stories in Exodus and Numbers the objects of the people's murmuring were usually Moses and Aaron. On only three occasions did Moses alone receive the flack (Exod. 15:24; 17:3; Num. 15:36), and only once is Aaron mentioned by himself (Num. 16:11). Yet in two stories Moses himself was also the reason for the complaint, because members in the group rebelled against his authority and office. The one case is the rebellion of Korah and friends who rose against Moses and Aaron because of their "holier-than-thou" attitudes (Num. 16:3). The particular complaint of Eliab's sons, Dathan and Abiram, "that you must also make yourself a prince over us" (16:13) is strikingly reminiscent of the question of the Hebrew slaves whose quarreling Moses tried to settle the day after he killed the Egyptian. In fact, that early question "Who made you a prince and a judge over us?" (Exod. 2:14) seems to prefigure the troubles Moses would experience later with his own people. In the case of Korah's challenge, Moses set the stage for a verdict concerning "who is holy," and the answer came when the earth swallowed alive Korah and his company of rebels.

The second challenge to Moses' authority came from Aaron himself and Miriam. The story at Numbers 12:1–16 does not read smoothly, and one suspects there are two issues at stake: (1) Moses' marriage to a Cushite woman, and (2) Moses' exclusive claim as the Lord's spokesman.

The problem of marriage to the Cushite raises several questions. In the first place, what in fact is a Cushite? Elsewhere in the Old Testament the term refers to the people and territory in the southern Nile Valley, below Egypt (e.g., Isa. 11:11; 20:3–5; 43:3). The term is translated in the Septuagint as "Ethiopia." Because this area is far removed from Moses and the wilderness area, scholars have suggested that "Cush" in Numbers 12 should be read as "Cushan" which is parallel to Midian at Habakkuk 3:7. In that case, the passage could

refer to Zipporah, the Midianite woman whom Moses married earlier
(Exod. 2:21). Second, what is the reason for the complaint by
Miriam and Aaron? If the woman in Numbers 12:1 were a Midianite,
then the issue is the attitude which the Israelites had toward Midianites in the stories of the wilderness and of the land settlement. That
group of people joined with Moabites to hire Balaam to curse Israel
(Num. 22), for which they were appropriately punished (Num. 31).
The hatred of Midianites was so great that when the man Zimri took
one of their women into his tent, the priest Phinehas slew both of
them in order to avoid a plague (Num. 25:1ff.). On the other hand,
if the woman whom Moses married in the wilderness were an Ethi-
opian, then she was probably black, and the issue was thus interracial
marriage. In this case, the punishment recorded in verses 9–15 contains a touch of irony. Miriam became "snow white" with a form of
leprosy.

More clear is the challenge by Aaron and Miriam to the uniqueness of Moses' role as mediator or spokesman between Yahweh and
the people (12:2). Just as in the case of Korah's challenge to Moses'
authority as leader, so here Yahweh himself intervened in order to
settle the issue. In an encounter at the door of the tent of meeting,
Yahweh spoke out of the pillar of cloud that he makes himself known
to prophets (Miriam is called a prophetess at Exod. 15:20) by means
of dreams and visions, but he speaks to his "servant Moses" clearly,
even "mouth to mouth," and appears to Moses' sight alone (vv. 7–8).

On the one hand, the account in Numbers 12:2–8 puts Aaron and
Miriam in their place—behind and under Moses. On the other hand,
in its present context the story seems to function as a corrective to a
possible misunderstanding from the previous chapter. In 11:24–30
Moses took seventy elders of the camp community out to the tent of
meeting where the Lord appeared in the cloud. There Yahweh took
some of Moses' spirit of prophecy and placed it on the elders, giving
them one shot at prophecy. Meanwhile, back at the camp the spirit
landed on two men Eldad and Medad, and they prophesied too.
When reports of this episode came to Moses, Joshua urged the leader
to forbid it. But Moses responded with his famous remark, "Would
that all the Lord's people were prophets, . . ." (v. 29). While the text
is used as a classic pericope for preaching about the witnessing of all
believers, it nevertheless seemed necessary for the compiler to follow

the story with 12:2–8 where Yahweh reasserted that his relationship with Moses was unique. It seems indeed that while elsewhere Moses is considered to be the prophet par excellence (Deut. 34:10), in the present text he is contrasted with prophets by his title "servant" (Num. 12:7).

The negative view of the wilderness is attested frequently throughout the Old Testament. In the Book of Deuteronomy this rebellion of the people is given as the reason why Moses was not allowed to enter the Promised Land (cf. 3:26; 4:21); the testing of the Lord by the people at Massah seems to provide the paradigm for rebellion in general (6:16). In the historical summary at Psalm 106, the wilderness is described solely in negative terms: the people rebelled again and again in spite of the gracious and saving deeds of Yahweh. Likewise Psalm 78 contrasts the love and care of Yahweh (from the exodus through the wilderness into the land) with the constant sin and rebellion of the people. And at Ezekiel 20:10ff. the wilderness experience is nothing but grievous rebellion by the people against God.

This entire interpretation of the wilderness as a period of rebellion has come to be termed "the murmuring motif." The origin and reason for the motif has been explained in several ways. Among a variety of options, those by Simon de Vries and George W. Coats are particularly interesting. De Vries argues that the tradition developed in order to explain the lapse of time necessary to move Israel from the south to an eastern entrance to the land and to explain Israel's earlier defeat as a consequence of her rebellion (*JBL* 87 [1968] 51ff.). Coats suggests that the primary traditions about the wilderness are positive and that the negative or "murmuring" texts first appear in the J document of Jerusalem as a polemic against the traditions of the northern kingdom. Psalm 78 provides Coats with his strongest evidence, for after the experiences (traditions?) of Ephraim are described negatively as the people's rebellion, the psalm concludes by celebrating the elections of Judah, Mount Zion, and David (*Rebellion in the Wilderness*). Coats's view has much to commend it, although it is indeed difficult to establish with certainty that the positive wilderness traditions are earlier than the negative. The written evidence simply does not bear out this sequence.

As we have discussed the wilderness tradition here, following essentially the position of Brevard Childs, the narratives in Exodus and

Numbers attest consistently to the "murmuring" of the people. Yet before the golden calf incident at Sinai, the murmuring arose out of a particular and legitimate need, and so the Lord's response was one of gracious care and guidance. After the apostasy at Mount Sinai, when the relationship between the Lord and people was shaken, the murmuring came without legitimate need, and so the Lord's response was one of anger and judgment. In neither case do the people come up smelling like roses, but in both cases—before and after Sinai— the Lord continued to guide the delivered people to the land which he promised the fathers long before.

What is striking in these murmurings of the people in the wilderness is the consistent denial on their part of the exodus deliverance. With disgusting regularity the Israelites wished the exodus had never occurred (Exod. 16:3; 17:3; Num. 11:20; 14:2; 20:4–5; 21:5), an attitude which they expressed first at the sea itself (Exod. 14:11–12). Yet even while they denied God's salvation as it was taking place and as they looked back upon it, the Lord continued to lead them on to fulfill his promises. Nowhere, it seems, is the Yahwist's contention throughout his entire story made more obvious than in the wilderness tradition: Yahweh continues his fidelity to his promises, not because of, but in spite of his people. The fulfillment of all that Yahweh promised is due exclusively to his own action.

The wilderness is the time between the saving event and the entrance into the Promised Land. In the Christian life, wilderness is the time between the death and resurrection of Jesus Christ and his coming again to consummate the kingdom. During the "in between time" God cares for physical and spiritual needs as he continues to lead us on even when, in our subtle ways, we deny his salvation and otherwise murmur because of our wants rather than our needs.

CHAPTER EIGHT

THEOPHANY AND COVENANT

To isolate one specific statement from the confessional histories in order to zero in on the Sinai tradition—as we did with the "bring out" formula of the exodus tradition—is impossible simply because Sinai is not mentioned explicitly in the historical surveys. As early as 1938 Gerhard von Rad noted the absence of Sinai in those historical "credos" and concluded that originally Sinai, a cult festival associated with the Feast of Tabernacles at Shechem, was separate from the exodus-conquest traditions associated with the Feast of Weeks at Gilgal (see *Problem of the Hexateuch and Other Essays,* pp. 1–78). The lively amplification of and debate over von Rad's thesis has been described cogently by E. W. Nicholson (*Exodus and Sinai*) and so, although von Rad's suggested separation of exodus and Sinai has by no means been adequately refuted, we are not justified in devoting space and time to a treatment of the problem here.

What von Rad's study raises for our concerns is the nature of the Sinai material itself. In this body of tradition from Exodus 19 through Leviticus to Numbers 10:32, diversity rules supreme—as it does in Sinai/Horeb stories elsewhere. In order to make some attempt at organizing these diverse elements, I have chosen to deal here with Sinai in terms of theophany and covenant.

SINAI AS THEOPHANY

1. *Exodus 24:1a, 9–11.* Yahweh instructed Moses to bring up on the mountain Aaron, the brothers Nadab and Abihu, and seventy of the elders. When the entourage arrived at the appropriate spot, "they saw the God of Israel." No harm came to them, as one might expect of those who lay their eyes on God (cf. Exod. 33:20), and so "they beheld God, and ate and drank" (v. 11).

The account is startling because of its repeated and blatant reference to seeing God. Such claims are rare indeed in the Old Testament, being reserved elsewhere for visionary experiences of individuals who are about to be called as prophets (Isa. 6:1ff.) or who are given prophetic messages (1 Kings 22:19ff.). Usually theophanies ("God-appearances") are camouflaged in the Old Testament by clouds, darkness, smoke, noise, and whatever else might make clear that one sees the signs of his presence rather than Yahweh himself. Moreover in virtually every theophany in the Hebrew Bible, the action moves quickly from what the people see to what God says. Yet here at Exodus 24:9–11, none of these cautions is taken: twice, we are told, the entourage "saw God." No signs. No speaking. They saw God.

And yet, true to theophanies elsewhere in the Bible, God himself is not described. What is given is a description of that on which he stood: "under his feet it was like a product of sapphire stone and like the substance of heaven for clarity" (v. 10). Apparently, at their position on Mt. Sinai, the sacred place, the seventy-four representatives of Israel had a bird's-eye-view of God through the firmament. Like Jacob at Bethel (Gen. 28:10–17), they were standing at the navel of the earth where the divine and human worlds merge.

Having survived the awe-ful sight, the men of Israel "ate and drank." In light of the custom attested elsewhere that human beings establish a covenant by dining together (cf. Gen. 26:26–33; Josh. 9:3–15), many scholars interpret this meal on the mountain as a covenant-making rite which brings into relationship God and Israel. Recently, E. W. Nicholson has raised objection to this interpretation on the grounds that elsewhere meals—even cultic meals—are eaten in the presence of God without implying a covenant (see Deut. 12:7; 14:26; 27:7; 1 Chron. 29:22; and esp. Exod. 18:12). The meal then might simply be a means of rejoicing. If this understanding is correct —as seems likely—then the account at 24:9–11 is throughout a theophany text (see *Exodus and Sinai,* pp. 68–70; *VT* 24 [1974] 77–97).

This tradition of Sinai, in which only the seventy elders of Israel are often considered to be the original characters of the story, seems to be quite early in the development of Sinai traditions. While it has variously been assigned to J and E, serious problems with either choice make it likely that the story is an ancient tradition from an unknown source.

2. *Exodus 19:9–20; 20:18–21*. Yahweh promised Moses that he would come in a thick cloud and speak to Moses so that the people might hear the conversation and believe Moses for ever (cf. 14:31). While Moses played no significant role in 24:9–11, here in chapter 19 his role is essential. Moses, following instructions, prepares for what is about to occur: people are consecrated, clothes laundered, bounds set around the mountain. According to the timetable, *"on the morning of the third day* there were thunders and lightnings, and a thick cloud upon the mountain, and a very loud trumpet blast, so that all the people who were in the camp trembled. Then Moses brought the people . . . to meet God; . . . *And Mount Sinai was wrapped in smoke, because the Lord descended upon it in fire; and the smoke of it went up like the smoke of a kiln, and the whole mountain quaked greatly.* And as the sound of the trumpet grew louder and louder, Moses spoke, and God answered him in thunder" (vv. 16–19; italics added).

Most scholars divide the text into the sources J and E: J represented by the italicized words above; E, by the remainder. When such a division is accepted, there are two theophanic descriptions of God's presence on Sinai: J portrays a volcanic eruption while E describes a storm. On the basis of J's volcanic portrayal, some have tried to locate Sinai in an area where volcanoes are known to have been active in the second half of the second millenium b.c. Although there is much evidence to locate Mt. Sinai in areas other than the traditional Jebel Musa in the southern Sinai peninsula (e.g., in the Seir region or east of Aqaba), the descriptions of both J and E seem more stereotypical than actual (cf. the description of Baal's theophany in Ugaritic texts which includes the quaking of mountains, thunder, clouds [see II AB vii 26–33 at *ANET,* p. 135]).

In all probability the action which originally followed Exodus 19:20 is that of 20:18–21. As the people experienced all this storm and volcanic (!) activity (the combination is due apparently to the JE redactor), they were afraid and backed away. Pushing Moses out in front, they ordered him to speak for God rather than allow them to hear God directly. In typical E fashion, Moses told the people that all this was a test from God to establish reverence among them "that you may not sin" (v. 20). Then Moses departed for the darkness while the people nestled in safety at a distance.

The account at Exodus 19:9–20 and 20:18–21 portrays Sinai as a theophany experience or tradition which established Moses as the necessary mediating spokesman between Yahweh/God and the people. The sequence of events in these passages and in the intervening material is as follows: (a) a theophany of storm and volcanic description, (b) God's speaking the Ten Commandments to all the people, (c) the people's request for a mediator to speak God's words rather than their hearing God directly. The second action, that of God's speaking to all the people, derives from the transition from chapter 19 to 20: at the end of 19 Moses went down from the mountain to the people, and in the first verse of chapter 20 God spoke the commandments. Since Moses was no longer with God on the mountain, the divine address must have been directed to all the people. (*The Jerusalem Bible* notes the unevenness here by ending chapter 19 with three dots.)

This threefold action of theophany, Decalogue, and plea for intercessor is spelled out more smoothly and more precisely at Deuteronomy 4:9–14; 5:1–21, 22–33. The author of this piece explains that the plea for the mediator came about after "the Lord spoke to all your assembly" (5:22). The people recognized that once was enough: "if we hear the voice of Yahweh our God any more, we shall die" (5:25). Therefore they sent Moses for any further communications, and the Lord commended the people for their wise decision (5:28–29). It seems that the author of this section of Deuteronomy held to the same theological position as the editor who gave to Exodus 19—20 its present form. The purpose of the whole scheme is to explain to the people of God that Yahweh no longer speaks directly to them; rather he speaks through mediators—at the wise suggestion of the people themselves back at Sinai/Horeb. The message of the scheme is no less valid for even our own day when God seems to be silent in contrast to his "obvious actions" and "audible words" of the good old days: he speaks now through messengers.

Thus, in contrast to the blatant theophany of Exodus 24:9–11, that of chapter 19 seems to serve as a foil against which or out of which the emphasis is on God's speaking his will and on the use of a mediator for future communication. In this understanding, theophany itself becomes de-emphasized in order to pave the way for God's *tôrāh* (i.e., his instruction). It is precisely in this development that the theophany of the Song of Moses at Deuteronomy 33 can be understood: first theophany in verse 2, then law (*tôrāh*) in verse 4.

3. *Exodus 24:15b–18.* In a somewhat different way the Priestly writer provides us with the same sequence. At Exodus 24:15b–18 the exilic theologian describes theophany in terms of the glory of the Lord appearing in a cloud. The phenomenon was seen "for six days" on Mount Sinai; then the Lord spoke "on the seventh day," summoning Moses to enter the cloud and ascend the mountain. During a forty-day period, the Lord gave to Moses cultic instructions regarding the tabernacle, the ark, altar, priesthood, atonement, and the like. The emphasis for the Priest in the theophany-*tôrāh* sequence is not to enhance the mediatorial role of Moses but to explain that the glory of the Lord moved with the people from Sinai to Jerusalem where the tabernacle was replaced by the temple (cf. Exod. 40:34–38). In this way the glory of the Lord, first attested in the wilderness when the Lord came speaking the promise of food (Exod. 16:10–12), became a continuous experience for the people of Israel to whom the Lord communicated his will and presence throughout the wilderness wanderings (see Num. 20:6ff.) and eventually in the Jerusalem temple (see Ezek. 8:4).

This theophany description of 24:15b–18 later took on christological significance in the New Testament. The Sinai revelation serves as the basis for the Transfiguration Story at Mark 9:2–9 and parallels. There on a mountain the voice which spoke out of the cloud related not detailed cultic instructions but a brief announcement regarding Jesus' identity. The divine statement "This is my son, the beloved; listen to him" settles the christological question which began in Mark 8:27: "Who do men say that I am?" (See McCurley, *JBL* 93 [1974] 67–81.)

SINAI AS COVENANT

One cannot leave the narrative portions of Exodus 19—34 without direct contact with the concept of covenant (*bᵉrît*). Throughout the patriarchal stories the covenant was the oath to which God obligated himself to the promises of posterity, land, and blessing. Now at Sinai, covenant becomes prominent once again, but the understanding of covenant takes a different form.

Immediately after the Priest's brief itinerary at Exodus 19:1–2 occurs a classic covenant passage. Verses 3–8 are often said to follow the pattern of suzerain-vassal treaties known from the royal archives of the Hittites whose empire lasted from approximately 1500 to 1200 B.C. Parallels between these Hittite treaties and Old Testament covenant texts were first demonstrated by George Mendenhall in his *Law and Covenant in Israel and the Ancient Near East.* Following the work by Victor Korošec on Hittite treaties (1931), Mendenhall brought to biblical study the following elements of ancient treaties.

Preamble naming the parties involved.

Historical prologue describing the past relations of the two parties.

Stipulations imposed on the vassal, primary of which was exclusive loyalty to the "great king" (i.e. the Hittite).

Blessings and curses listed for the vassal, dependent of course on loyalty to the suzerain.

Calling upon the gods of both parties as witnesses to the treaty.

Provisions for reading a copy regularly to remind the parties of their responsibilities.

Theologically, the covenant formula in the Old Testament insists on the priority of God's action over his demands for obedience. To put it in other terms, God's Indicative always precedes God's Imperative. The history of God's redeeming activity with his people is the basis—not the consequence—of the people's responsibility. It is true in the New Testament as in the Old, as the structure of the Pauline epistles demonstrates. This theological sequence is perhaps the reason why the treaty formula could be adapted to the biblical faith and used in certain texts.

1. *The historical prologue.* It is, of course, not primarily form but content in a given form that is the concern of a theological examination of the Scriptures. And so we turn to Exodus 19:3–8 for a look at some of the key expressions. The speech of Yahweh begins much like a prophetic messenger formula: "Thus you shall say . . ." (see, e.g., Jer. 10:11). The "historical prologue" itself seems to consist of three parts. (a) The reference to the exodus event is stated as an eyewitness formula "you have seen" which is so common in the Deuteronomistic corpus (see Deut. 29:1ff.; Josh. 24:7; cf. Deut. 11:2ff.). (b) The historical summary continues with "and I bore you on eagles'

wings." Often in the Psalms the image of being under the wings (of
the eagle) indicates the Lord's protection of the individual from harm
(Pss. 17:8; 36:7; 57:1; 63:7; 91:4); in prophetic texts the eagle
image appears to describe a warrior, presumably Yahweh (see Jer.
48:40; 49:22; Ezek. 17:3, 7). But the idea of Yahweh carrying Israel
on eagles' wings is paralleled elsewhere only at Deuteronomy 32:10–
12, where it refers to the Lord's guidance of the people through the
wilderness. (c) The last part of the historical prologue, "and brought
you in to me," is strikingly reminiscent of the "bring out-bring in"
formula of the confessional histories which described the exodus and
the land settlement with one sweep. The "bring in" (*hēbî'*) seems thus
to speak of Yahweh's presence in Canaan rather than on Sinai (cf.
Deut. 4:38; 6:10, 23; 7:1; 8:7; 9:4, 28; 11:29; 26:9; 30:5; 31:20f.).
Thus the threefold historical summary of Exodus 19:4 describes the
exodus-wilderness-conquest tradition which we have already discussed in the confessional histories, and the description itself is strikingly similar to the language and imagery of the Deuteronomistic
corpus.

2. *Covenant Stipulations.* The stipulations of obeying the Lord and
keeping his covenant strike one as a bolt out of the blue, particularly
because of the conditional "if." Unlike the covenant which God made
with the patriarchs in which he obligated himself and placed no conditions on the humans, here he obligates Israel to keep his covenant
(still to be concluded) and states the relationship conditionally (see
the interpretation of Sinai/Horeb at Deut. 4:12). The covenant is
now more of a contract than an oath. While it does not contradict the
earlier covenant with the patriarchs, it does stand in tension with that
promise (see Bright, *Covenant and Promise,* esp. pp. 24–43). Nevertheless, the use of the conditional "if" does not eliminate the priority
of God's activity; nor does it invalidate that act. In this text, Yahweh's
deliverance and guidance have already occurred. Now, however, in
order to experience the blessings promised, Israel is to meet certain
conditions (for similar use of "if" ['*im*] see Deut. 8:19; 13:18; 28:1,
2, 15, 58; 30:10.)

3. *Covenant blessings.* The blessings for obedience and covenant
fidelity are glorious indeed, but full of responsibility. Israel's blessing
will be threefold: the Lord will make her (a) "my own special treas-

ure" (*s^egullâ*), (b) "a kingdom of priests" (*mamleket kôh^anîm*) and (c) "a holy nation" (*gôy qādôš*). Individually and collectively these terms deserve particular attention.

(a) That Israel will become Yahweh's *s^egullâ* in the midst of all other peoples who belong to God is a statement both about Israel and about Yahweh. Translations attempt to capture the meaning of the word in the following ways: "my special possession" (*NAB, NEB*), "my very own" (*JB*), "my own people" (*TEV*); perhaps best of all is "My treasured possession" (*The Torah,* JPS). A *s^egullâ* is the treasure which belongs to a king apart from that which he possesses by right of his rule; it is his private treasure in the midst of his public domain (for this precise use of the common Semitic term in the Old Testament, see 1 Chron. 29:3). Israel is to be Yahweh's private treasure in the midst of the universe over which he is King. Thus the term defines both Israel and Yahweh.

(b) The understanding of Yahweh as King leads directly to Israel's role in his kingdom: she is to be "a kingdom of priests." Apparently the expression is intended to define further the privilege given to Israel over all other peoples; Israel can draw near to Yahweh as priests do. At the same time, this priestly role carried with it the responsibility of bearing the judgment of others before God (Exod. 28:29–30) and of maintaining the requirements for holiness (Lev. 21).

(c) In light of the responsibility of priests to be holy, the third blessing takes on particular significance: you shall be my "holy nation." That Israel became a special nation (*gôy*) on the basis of this covenant at Sinai, or that she became a nation at all, is not unrelated to that promise to Abraham with which Yahweh's history with the Hebrews began: "I will make of you a great nation" (*gôy gādôl,* Gen. 12:2). The qualifying adjective "holy" (*qādôš*) at Exodus 19:6 expresses Israel's separateness out of all other peoples; in this specific context the separateness is defined by the other expressions "my special treasure" and "a kingdom of priests" in all the earth which belongs to the Lord.

While the expression "a kingdom of priests" occurs nowhere else in the Hebrew Old Testament, the combination of "my special treasure" and "a holy nation" appears several times. At Deuteronomy 7:6; 14:2; 26:18–19 the combination occurs, but with one significant difference: the "holy nation" (*gôy qādôš*) is changed to "holy people" (*'am qādôš*). The responsibilities of living out existence as Yahweh's *sᵉgullâ* and *gôy/'am qādôš* are always related to the keeping of his commandments, statutes, and ordinances. The conditional "obey my voice and keep my covenant" at Exodus 19:5 probably points forward to the Decalogue and the Book of the Covenant which follow in chapters 20—23. At Deuteronomy 7:6–11 the election terms are followed by a characteristic "therefore": be careful to do the commandment, and the statutes, and the ordinances (v. 11). The same is true at Deuteronomy 14:1–2 and 26:16–19. It seems therefore that the Indicative of Yahweh's deliverance of Israel and his election of her to be his own treasure is always followed by his Imperative to live up to the responsibilities that deliverance and election include. To put it another way, to be God's private treasure and his holy nation/people is to be obedient to the Lord as the sovereign King.

The threefold blessing of "my special treasure," "a kingdom of priests," and "a holy nation," while unique in the Hebrew Bible, appears again in the Septuagint at Exodus 23:22. Here, at the end of the Book of the Covenant, the conditional "if" is directly related to the preceding stipulations.

However, it is the use of this blessing formula in the New Testament which is especially instructive for Christians. At 1 Peter 2:9 the phrases are addressed to Christians who are considered to be exiles (see 1:1, 17; 2:11; cf. also James 1:1; Phil. 3:20). Christians are exiles in the world not in a sociological but in a theological sense: "born anew to a living hope through the resurrection of Jesus Christ from the dead" (1:3), "through the living and abiding word of God" (1:23; cf. 2:2). These exiles who are in but not of the world are, like the exiles of the Old Testament, "a chosen race, a royal priesthood, a holy nation, God's own people"—but there is no "if" about it! The status has already been accomplished by God's own act in Jesus Christ. Nevertheless, the Imperative follows. The content of this Imperative, however, is not the keeping of commandments and ordinances but "that you may declare his praises." This quotation from Isaiah 43:21 defines the response of the exiles of Babylon when the Lord delivers them from the foreign land by a new exodus (see vv. 16–20). The responsive declaration of Christians seems to include both the preaching of the gospel which they received (1:25) and

conduct in the world which testifies to their election as a holy people
(see 2:11–12; 4:1–6).

4. *Covenant making and covenant renewal.* The sequel to Exodus
19:3–8 is the covenant-making rite at 24:3–8. In the present context
the reference to Moses' writing down the words of Yahweh points
back to the instructions of the Book of the Covenant (20:22—
23:22) which Moses then read to the people (24:7). The repeated
response of the people vowing their obedience (vv. 3, 7) ties the passage closely to their vow at 19:8 and to the conditions of the covenant
introduced at 19:5. The primary action at 24:3–8 is the concluding
of that covenant mentioned earlier by means of a blood ceremony.
Moses sent "young men" from among the people to offer burnt offerings and peace sacrifices to the Lord. The blood in which is the life
(Lev. 17:10–16) was used for ritual purposes. It was thrown against
the altar here and elsewhere (Lev. 3:2, 13; Deut. 12:27) while apparently the meat was eaten, as a means of establishing communion
of the people with God and among themselves (cf. Lev. 19:5–6).
This fellowship was possible, it seems, because the blood on the altar
effected atonement for the people (Lev. 17:11).

While the atoning blood and eating of meat accomplished fellowship in the believing community, it is only here at Exodus 24:8 and
in an allusion to the event at Zechariah 9:11 that blood was used in a
covenant-making rite. At the Last Supper of Jesus with his disciples,
however, the relationship of blood and new covenant is stated explicitly: "This is my blood of the covenant, which is poured out for
many" (Mark 14:24), to which Matthew adds "for the forgiveness
of sins" (Matt. 26:28). Even Paul's proclamation of the tradition
which he received from the risen Lord attests to this relationship:
"This cup is the new covenant in my blood" (1 Cor. 11:25). Thus
while Israel was forbidden to drink the blood in which was the life,
Christians drink of the cup and eat bread in order to "proclaim the
Lord's death until he comes" (1 Cor. 11:26) and to effect the forgiveness of sins for many (i.e., for all) which was accomplished by the
pouring out of his blood, not on a sacrificial altar but on an unholy hill.

Somewhere in the midst of complex redaction, Exodus 34 seems
to contain the Yahwist's account of the covenant making on Mt.
Sinai. The covenant (see v. 10) contains at present a Decalogue (the
so-called Ritual Decalogue, vv. 11–28) which Moses brought down

from the mountain and presented to the people (vv. 29–32). Yet in the present context of the whole Sinai narrative the covenant from the J source is now a renewal of the covenant, and the two tables a second copy. For between the covenant-making rite at the foot of the mountain, recorded at 24:3–8, and the covenant made on top of the mountain in the presence of Moses alone (34:10) occurred the act of rebellion par excellence: Israel made the golden calf (chap. 32).

Even while Moses was on the mountain receiving the tables of law which by either account (Exod. 20 or 34) demanded exclusive worship of Yahweh, the people below enticed Aaron to make them gods to lead them. They claimed they did not know what happened to Moses, and they were no longer sure of the credibility of the invisible Yahweh. The people rejected the man Moses "who brought us up out of the land of Egypt" in favor of Aaron's molten calf about whom the people exclaimed "These are your gods, O Israel, who brought you up out of the land of Egypt" (34:4).

The parallels of this incident with the account of Jeroboam's construction of two sanctuaries at Bethel and Dan, recorded at 1 King 12:25ff., have been discussed often. Most striking is the confession "Behold your gods, O Israel . . ." at 1 Kings 12:28. In each story an altar is built (Exod. 32:5; 1 Kings 12:32, 33). and sacrifices are offered on the altars (Exod. 32:5–6; 1 Kings 12:32). In both stories Levites are clear of all guilt (Exod. 32:25–29; 1 Kings 12:31). God is greatly displeased (Exod. 32:10; 1 Kings 13:2), and the calf or the altar is destroyed (Exod. 32:29; 1 Kings 13:5).

It has been argued that the original story is the act of Jeroboam in the tenth century B.C. and that the priests of Jerusalem composed the story in Exodus 32 to demonstrate the Lord's displeasure with such calves and the eventual destruction of the sanctuaries. Serious questions have been raised about this interpretation. The point of Jeroboam's act and the Deuteronomist's unfavorable judgment is not the calves as much as the rivalry to the Jerusalem cult (see 1 Kings 12: 26–28). In fact, when the judgment came (1 Kings 13:5; 2 Kings 23:15), no mention is made of calves; rather the altar at Bethel was crushed to dust (cf. Exod. 32:20). It seems that the accusation of making calves and the claim "Behold your gods . . ." were taken from the Sinai story and inserted, perhaps by the Deuteronomist (cf. Deut. 9:13–21), into 1 Kings 12 in order to identify Jeroboam's setting up rival sanctuaries with the grave rebellion of Aaron. Thus, while Exodus 32 seems to be affected at many points with Deuteronomistic redaction and insertion, the calf episode itself belongs to Sinai traditions originally.

In spite of the literary complexities of Exodus 32—34, the record of the people making a molten image at the same time Moses was receiving the Decalogue in written form points to the frailty of the people with whom God made his covenant. Over against the tables of law which were the visible product of God (31:18; 32:16), the visible image of the calf was the product of human impatience and religious license. As such, it could have spelled the end for Israel. Thus the Sinai covenant differs from that made with Abraham. In the covenant with the patriarchs in which God obligated himself, his own fidelity pointed forward to the certain fulfillment of his promises. In the Sinai covenant in which God placed the obligations on Israel, the continuation of the relationship is not certain. The people merited only God's judgment and destruction because of the calf they had made. Only by the intervention of Moses and the grace of God (32:11–14), the judgment of God which followed (32:35) did not annihilate the people but led instead to covenant renewal (chap. 34).

It is for reason of this frailty, and indeed inability, of the people to be faithful that Paul contrasted the Mosaic covenant as "the dispensation of condemnation" with "the dispensation of righteousness" which is the new covenant in Christ (2 Cor. 3). Or to contrast allegorically Hagar as the Sinai covenant resulting in slavery with Sarah as the covenant of promise which results in freedom. For Paul considered Christians to be not the children of Moses but "like Isaac . . . children of promise" (Gal. 4:21–31). It is only when God takes the obligation on himself that we become his children in Christ Jesus through faith (Gal. 3:23–29). Thus while the Tetrateuch kept both types of covenant in tension, Paul clearly chose between them for Christians.

CHAPTER NINE

COMMAND AND PRESENCE

In the Old Testament itself, the law given on Sinai through Moses is not that which condemns but rather that which the Lord gives graciously to his redeemed people in order to guide them to life and to provide for his presence. The collection of law codes at Exodus 20—23, 25—31, 35—40, the Book of Leviticus, and Numbers 1—10 is the Imperative of God's will which follows the Indicative of his deliverance from Egypt. This extended body of instruction explains for Israel not only how she is to live as the redeemed of the Lord but also how God will continue to be present throughout generations.

THE DIVINE COMMAND

1. *The Decalogue.* The general context of the Decalogue at Exodus 20:1-17, close to the beginning of the Sinai tradition, is sufficient to regard it as an Imperative following the Indicative of the exodus event in Exodus 1—15. However, the Decalogue itself strengthens this impression by the specific prologue to the Ten Words at verse 2: "I am Yahweh your God, who brought you out of the land of Egypt, out of the house of bondage." What follows then is God's will for the people he has already saved.

While most scholarly interest in the Decalogue has concentrated on the nature, date, and origin of the type of law, a more productive approach is one treating the structure of decalogues. Hartmut Gese suggests that decalogues consist of five pairs of commands. After demonstrating such pairs in Leviticus 19:13-18; Deuteronomy 27:15-26; Exodus 22:18-31, he turns his attention to Exodus 20:1-17. On the basis of strong textual support in the Septuagint, Philo, New Testament (cf. Romans 13:9; Luke 18:20) and especially in the second/first century B.C. Hebrew text of the Nash Papyrus, Gese suggests transposing the commandments regarding killing (Exod. 20:

13) and adultery (20:14). By this likely transposition, the Decalogue treats five areas of life in apodictic style ("Thou shalt/shalt not"):

(1) God, his exclusiveness and personalness (20:3, 4–6)
(2) Cult and sabbath, representing the realm of holiness in which humans can participate (20:7, 8–11)
(3) Family, the sphere from which people descend (20:12, 14)
(4) Humanness, the free life of people (20:13, 15)
(5) Social life, the protection of the fellow-citizen, his rights and property (20:16, 17)

This structure reveals a comprehensive system extending from God to fellow-citizen. The completeness is accomplished with the characteristic biblical notion of forming a totality out of two parallel or opposed terms. And so, by this structural arrangement the Decalogue witnesses to God's concern for all of life by his gift of law to his redeemed people.

Just as the Decalogue of Exodus 20 was given in the context of making the covenant (i.e., between 19:3–8 and 24:3–8), so the Decalogue at Exodus 34:11–26 was granted when the covenant was renewed (34:10). This second, so-called "ritual" decalogue earns the title "ten words" only because of the explicit reference to "the ten commandments" at verse 28. Apart from that assistance, it is difficult to enumerate ten laws in verses 11–26 of the present text. In any case, the laws here—again in apodictic style—concentrate first on the exclusive worship of Yahweh (v. 14, almost lost by a parenthesis in the present context) with its parallel forbidding molten images (v. 17), and then on such ritual matters as feasts with appropriate and inappropriate offerings (vv. 18–26). The presupposition of an agricultural life indicates settlement in the land of Canaan.

2. *The Book of the Covenant.* The title for the code of law at Exodus 20:22—23:33 derives from mention of "the book of the covenant" which Moses read to the people in the covenant-making ceremony of 24:3–8. Whether the code was inserted at this point because of the reference in 24:7 or the title of the book was given because of the prior existence of the code, is difficult to argue with certainty. While the former option seems probable, the more important issues for our study are a) the type of law attested here, b) the likely origin of the code from a place and time other than that suggested by its present context, c) the revision of the code at a later

period in Israel's history, and d) the use of the code within the theological context of covenant making.

a. The type of law in this code is known as casuistic, a form of law known and used for centuries in the legal codes of the ancient Babylonians, Assyrians, and Hittites. Both in form and in content, many of these laws are similar to other ancient legal expressions (cf. Exod. 21:22–25 with Code of Hammurabi 196, 200, *ANET,* p. 175). Similarities do not indicate borrowing but commonality, that is, ancient Israel was part of the environment in which she lived. And so, while some of the laws in this collection are related specifically to Israel's faith, others are regulations of more common concern and thus akin to the laws of her neighbors.

b. The law code here presupposes a settled agricultural life during the period of the judges. The use of oxen (21:28—22:4), references to fields, vineyards, and grain (22:5–6), to harvest and winepresses (22:29), the sabbath rest for fields (22:10–11), agricultural feasts (22:14–18) and offering of firstfruits (22:19)—all these point to a time when Israel was settled in the land of Canaan and naturally concerned with laws concerning the land and its use. On the other side, there exists in this code no evidence of kingship or of later institutions which developed under the monarchies of Israel and Judah. Nor is there any reference to economic systems of the later period. Thus it seems that the law originated between the time of the settlement in Canaan and the establishment of the monarchy under David about 1000 B.C. Martin Noth has even argued that the code was the amphictyonic law which governed the tribal league during this period.

c. This law code, like any other one, was addressed to the particular situation out of which it originated. Any system of laws is written for the conditions of its own day, and when those conditions change, the laws must be updated, modernized, and in some cases reconstructed. The Book of the Covenant was updated within the Old Testament itself: in the code at Deuteronomy 12—26. A comparison of many of the laws in these codes shows that the Deuteronomic law of the seventh century B.C. was both an expansion and a modernizing of the older code. For example, the agricultural year of release at Exodus 23:10–11 is extended at Deuteronomy 15:1–11 to include financial debt. Likewise the law at Exodus 21:1–11 concerning purchase of slaves and length of enslavement is updated at Deuteronomy

15:12–18 to include the enslavement of a previously free person for economic reasons. The change in both these sets of laws is due to the increasing importance of a monetary economy in the course of Israel's social development. Gerhard von Rad lists nineteen such cases in which laws in the Book of the Covenant have parallels—usually from a later hand—in the Code of Deuteronomy (*Deuteronomy,* pp. 13–15). Such updating of laws even within the Old Testament itself should caution the present-day interpreter against absolutizing biblical laws.

d. While Israel employed the typical legal forms of the times, she used them all to ensure the exclusive relationship of the covenant between the Lord and herself. Israel interpreted her laws in the light of the God who acted in history to redeem his people and to unveil his jealous will, and so Israel lived against her environment at the same time that she lived in it. This context for laws within the theological framework of the covenant makes clear that for Israel there was no distinction between religious law and civil law. Where the church and state were essentially the same, all laws were believed to have had their origin in God who expressed his will for all areas of human life. Christians make the appropriate distinction between church and state, covenant community and world, and thus between religious and civil law. Unfortunately this distinction sometimes becomes such a separation that God is conveniently omitted from the world and limited in his concern to the church. Paul's exposition in Romans 13 is a helpful model for distinguishing without separating the church from the world with regard to law and authority.

3. *The Holiness Code.* The collection of laws at Leviticus 17:1—26:46 is generally agreed by scholars to represent an original unit. This body of statutes is called "the Holiness Code" simply because repeated confession of Yahweh's holiness forms the Indicative on which is based the Imperative to the people to be holy as well. To put it another way, God's holiness is to pervade the life of the people in all matters of ethics and ritual. The blessings for observing these laws and the curses for failing to do so bring the potpourri of statutes to a conclusion (26:3–43). Specifically the blessings for keeping the commandments are highlighted by the promise of God to confirm his covenant by making his abode among the people, walking among them, and being their God (vv. 9–12). The curses, as to be expected, involve terror, plagues, hunger, destruction, and finally exile. But the

bottom line is God's gracious promise that even though the people spurned him (v. 43), Yahweh will not spurn them (v. 44). Even in the land of exile, he will remember the covenant he made when he brought the people out of Egypt "that I might be their God: I am the Lord" (v. 45).

This conclusion to the Holiness Code is significant in two ways. In the first place, it enables us to determine that while many diverse segments of the code are more ancient than the whole, the collection became a reality during the exile of the sixth century B.C., perhaps after experiencing several stages of edition. In the second place, the conclusion sets the whole code into a particular perspective: Yahweh remembers the covenant with the people which he made at the deliverance from Egypt. That Yahweh became Israel's God in connection with the exodus is a prominent theme throughout the code (cf. 18:2; 19:36–37; 22:33; 23:43; 25:38, 55). Now at the conclusion, that relationship established first with the forefathers is the basis for the promise of divine remembrance in the new land of bondage, Babylon.

The claim of God's lordship over his people on the basis of the exodus makes clear to Israel that she became free in order to belong to him as servants (25:55). That they should not be slaves of Egypt (26:13) but servants of the Lord recalls the command from Yahweh to Pharaoh: "Let my son go that he may serve me" (Exod. 4:23). That deliverance or salvation has its goal in the worship and praise of God can be seen throughout the Bible (see Isa. 43:2, 25; 48:9–11; Phil. 2:5–11; 1 Peter 2:9–10). Therefore one is freed not to do his or her "own thing" but to give glory to God for his redemptive deeds.

So powerful is the authority of God as Israel's Lord that the divine claim "I am the Lord (your God)" punctuates one command after another (twenty-seven times in ten chapters). This exclusive claim on the people is the only indicative necessary for such diverse imperatives as keeping the statutes and ordinances (18:1–5; 22:31), avoiding the sexual abominations of other peoples (18:6–30), abstaining from idols (19:4), providing food for the hungry (19:9–10; 23:22), treating others justly and honestly (19:11–12, 13–14, 15–16, 35–36; 24:22), restoring one's property and freedom (25:15, 17), and even loving the neighbor and the stranger "as yourself" (19:17–18, 33–34).

This last imperative "to love your neighbor as yourself" has significance in the New Testament as well as here. It was said by Jesus to be the second great commandment, superseded only by the command to love God (see Mark 12:31 and parallels). In another place Jesus listed this command alongside five of the Ten Commandments as the means by which a certain young man might have eternal life (Matt. 19:19). For the apostle Paul the whole law is fulfilled in this one commandment to love the neighbor (Gal. 5:14). The importance ascribed to this commandment in the New Testament can be understood in the context of Leviticus 19 itself. Beginning at verse 13 and continuing through verse 18a there appears an apodictic series of ten commandments, all of which prescribe the means by which human beings relate to one another in community. The first four pairs (vv. 13–16) are stated negatively, that is, in terms of prohibitions. In the final pair each commandment presents the negative and positive sides of the same coin: "You shall not hate . . . but . . . reason" (v. 17); "you shall not take vengeance . . . but love your neighbor as yourself" (v. 18). The final command of the fifth pair of this decalogue sums up in a positive way the meaning of the preceding prohibitions regarding life in community: love. There follows immediately the divine claim "I am the Lord."

What makes this code unusual amidst the common claim of Yahweh to be Israel's God is the concern for holiness. The root of the Hebrew word *qādôš* means "separate," and so it is separateness from all else that defines "holy." Since only one is separate from everything, holiness belongs essentially to God. Yahweh's refrain "I am holy," however, is never an isolated claim, for in each instance God separated someone or something out of the profane everyday world in order to serve him and his purposes. On the basis of his holiness, Yahweh appointed Israel to be a holy people (19:2; 20:7, 26). Indeed God separated (*hibdîl*) Israel from the rest of peoples in order that she would belong to him, the Holy One (20:24–26). Moreover, within this holy people, God separated those who were to serve him and the people as priests; they too were to be holy (21:6–8, 15; 22:9, 32). Such a specific holy group was necessary in order to deal in the cult with holy things: separated for particular use was certain food (19:24; 22:3–4, 16) and specific days of convocation to the Lord (23:24, 27, 35–37).

The sanctity of Israel's worship by the institution of holy priests, holy things, and holy days was necessary in order to hallow and not profane Yahweh's holy name (22:2, 31–32). Such care was nothing less than a matter of life and death. To profane "the Name" or to "blaspheme the Name (of the Lord)" led to death (24:11–16, 23) or to exclusion from his presence (22:3). In either case, *shalom* was not possible, for life in its fullness is life in the presence of God.

THE DIVINE PRESENCE

Throughout the Tetrateuch the promise of God's presence with his chosen individuals and especially with his chosen people is a major theme. Moreover, precisely because it is a major theme covering several different sources and addressed to various times and places and conditions in Israel's life, the presence of God was constantly reinterpreted and thus took on various forms of expression.

From the very outset of his dealing with his people, God made his presence felt through his word, that is, he *spoke* his promises of blessing to Abraham, Isaac, and Jacob. More specifically, in several instances, God promised to a patriarch "I will be with you" (Gen. 26:3; 28:15; 46:4), or a patriarch confessed God's presence with him (Gen. 31:5; 35:3, cf. 50:25), or the narrator explained that the Lord's presence was with an individual (e.g., Joseph, Gen. 39:23).

God's promise of presence to Moses was manifested in Egypt by the plagues. Throughout the wilderness wanderings God's presence took the form of his continual provision for the needs of his people. More visibly, the Yahwist portrayed this presence of God in the pillar of cloud, and the Priest in terms of the glory of the Lord in a cloud. At Sinai God appeared in the theophanic signs of volcanic eruption (J), storm (E), and again as the glory of the Lord in a cloud (P).

In the instructions for establishing the cult, collected by the Priest and his successors in Exodus 25—31, 35—40 and Leviticus 1:1— Numbers 10:28, God provided the means for a continuing relationship and for his comforting presence with his people. The chapters from the Book of Exodus deal primarily with the presence of the glory of God in terms of the ark, the tabernacle, and the priesthood. Leviticus 1—7 is a code for sacrifices by which communion with the Lord might be realized, and chapters 8—10 tell how the consecrated priesthood can effect this fellowship in worship. Leviticus 11—16, a code for purification, shows how the holiness of God permeates all of life, and the Holiness Code, chapters 17—26, bases God's authoritative demand for holiness on his own nature. Finally, Numbers 1—10 explains how the people should be organized so that in their movement through time and space, God's presence might be manifest.

These codes of ritual laws seem to contain nothing significant for the Christian, loaded as they seem to be with ancient Israel's worship life. And yet these laws are nothing less than God's gracious gift to Israel, so that he might be present with them for all generations. As such, these provisions deserve some attention here.

1. *The Ark and the Tabernacle.* No sooner had Moses entered the cloud on the summit of Mt. Sinai than God began his long list of instructions for the building of "a sanctuary, that I may dwell in their midst" (Exod. 25:8). First is described the construction and purpose of a particular object within the sanctuary: the ark.

According to the instructions (Exod. 25:10–22) the ark was a portable box made of acacia wood which served as the container of the testimony or law. In this respect P followed the tradition in the Book of Deuteronomy which records that Moses placed in the ark the two tablets containing the Ten Commandments (Deut. 10:1–9). Because of its contents, the object was called the Ark of the Covenant or the Ark of the Testimony. Thus two relatively late traditions regard the ark as a receptacle for the law.

However, the Priest describes the ark in such a way that still another use of the object is identified: the throne of the presence of God. In 25:10–12 two cherubim are mentioned. The creatures were made of gold and were set facing each other while their wings covered the mercy seat. It was above this mercy seat that the Lord promised to meet with Moses and to speak his commandments for Israel. The cherubim themselves, winged creatures with lion bodies and human heads, were common in Canaan and with some modifications in Mesopotamia as guardians of a king's throne. Thus it seems that the ark represented a portable throne of the invisible God and was the special locale of his presence.

The notion of the ark as a throne is confirmed elsewhere. In the old Song of the Ark at Numbers 10:35–36, when the ark was picked up for transport, Moses addressed the "Lord" as though he were present as a king. Likewise the Narrative of the Ark in 1 Samuel 4—6 and 2 Samuel 6 describes the object as "the ark of the covenant of the Lord of hosts, who is enthroned on the cherubim" (1 Sam. 4:4; cf. also 2 Sam. 6:2; 2 Kings 19:15).

Thus, without debating here the original use of the ark in Israel's cult, we can observe two notions about the use and significance of the ark: as the container of law and as the throne of the invisible God. The only time the two functions occur in the same text is Exodus 25: 10–22 from the Priestly code.

As for the tabernacle itself, the structure described in Exodus 26 bears a striking resemblance to that of the later Jerusalem temple. For a nomadic sanctuary, this "tent of meeting" or "tent of testimony," as the Priest called it, was an elaborate structure made of wooden frames and measuring in cubits 30 by 10 by 10. Covered by skins of various sorts, the sanctuary was divided into several parts: one portion of the interior was sealed off as the Holy of Holies in which the ark was kept. Another area, the Holy Place, contained the candlestick and the table of shewbread (consecrated, unleavened bread). Outside the entrance stood the altar and the basin for washing. It seems indeed that the Priest combined the idea of an old nomadic sanctuary with the structure of the Jerusalem temple which stood from 960 B.C. until its destruction in 587 B.C. The Priest may indeed have been designing for the people the new temple to be constructed as part of Israel's restoration.

That old nomadic sanctuary, located outside the camp, originally had nothing to do with the ark (see Exod. 33:7–11), but the Priest combined the tent both with the camp (Num. 2:2, 17; cf. 5:2–3) and with the ark (Exod. 25). In this way the Priest made his testimony to the presence of God with his people, a presence which took the form of the glory of the Lord filling the tabernacle (Exod. 40:34–38) and traveling with his people from Sinai to Zion.

2. *The Priesthood.* The office of priest in the Old Testament is a complicated matter. The various classes or families of priests raise the most difficult questions. However, it is the major functions of priests that concern us here.

The Lord established the priesthood so that means might be provided for the people to have fellowship with himself. We have already seen in the Holiness Code that the priests were to be holy in order to keep pure the food and festivals which were set apart for the community's relationship with the holy God. Now we must examine: (a) those areas of responsibility in which the priests exercised their professional knowledge as teachers, (b) their roles in atoning for the people's sins, and (c) their responsibility to bless and to curse.

a. *The exercise of professional knowledge.* An important function for the priests was a medical one: the determination of a person's leprosy. The laws at Leviticus 13—14 are detailed in their instructions regarding the announcements "it is leprosy" (13:8) or "it is clean" (13:17). These diagnoses by the priests were, however, far more than medical; they had theological implications from beginning to end. First, the priest spoke on behalf of Yahweh who commissioned the priest to make such judgments and pronouncements. Second, the diagnosis determined whether or not a person was allowed to continue in the social and religious community (13:46; cf. 22:3–4) or to be reestablished when the disease was cured. Thus the opportunities to experience the presence of God in the cult were dependent upon the priests' professional knowledge and judgment.

In a slightly different sense the priests had the responsibility to teach the people the means by which ceremonial uncleanness might be avoided. On the basis of laws regarding bodily discharges due to sickness, nature, or pleasure, the priests could instruct the people specifically about keeping "separate from their uncleanness, lest they die in their uncleanness by defiling my tabernacle that is in their midst" (Lev. 15:31). Likewise, priestly instructions to the people about the proper distinctions between clean and unclean animals had as their purpose the consecration of the people before the holy God (Lev. 11; see especially vv. 44–45). Thus, precisely because the holy Lord was present in the community, such instructions served to keep the people safe from harm.

b. *The priestly role of atonement.* If the priest represented the Lord to the people in the exercise of professional knowledge, then in the role of atonement the priest represented the people. In the breastplate of judgment worn over his heart, Aaron (the priest) bore the names of the children of Israel when he entered the Holy Place in order to bring them into continual remembrance before Yahweh. By placing the Urim and Thummim into that breastplate, Aaron bore the judgment of the people on his heart before Yahweh (Exod. 28: 29–30). Moreover, an engraving which read "Holy to the Lord" and was fastened to the front of the priest's turban was the means by which the priest took upon himself any guilt incurred by the people in the holy offering. The purpose for this representation: that the people may be accepted by the Lord (Exod. 28:36–38). Thus by bearing in himself the names, the judgment, and the guilt of the people, the priest could maintain fellowship between the holy Lord and unholy people.

In a different way the priest made atonement for the unclean woman following childbirth (Lev. 12). As at the time of menstruation, a woman was considered to be unclean for a specified number of days. During this time she was not allowed to touch any hallowed thing or come into the sanctuary in order to experience the Lord's special presence there. When the days were completed, the woman would bring animals for a burnt offering and a sin offering to the priest at the door of the tent of meeting. The priest then offered it before the Lord, making atonement for her, and restoring her to the cultic community.

This atoning function was effective for the entire community once each year on the Day of Atonement. At this time the anointed and consecrated priest made atonement for himself, for all his family, for the holy place, for the tent of meeting, for the altar, and for all the people. In order to atone for himself and his family, the priest offered a sin offering and a burnt offering (Lev. 16:2–6, 11). The method of atoning for the holy place, the tent of meeting, and the altar was a blood-sprinkling rite (Lev. 16:15–19). Unlike the Priestly instruction at Exodus 28:29–30 where the priest bore the judgment of the people, here the iniquity of the people was transferred by the priest to a goat. Then the animal was sent out into the wilderness, thereby removing quite physically the taint of the community's sin (Lev. 16:20–22). The purpose of this atonement for the community was to remove all barriers to fellowship with Yahweh and to cleanse the people in his presence (16:30).

c. *The responsibility for blessing and curse.* The responsibility of the priest to pronounce and thus to effect curses on the people is attested in several places in the Old Testament (Deut. 27:13–26; Ps. 58:6–9). The clearest example in the Tetrateuchal laws occurs at Numbers 5:11–31 where is described the priest's role in the determination of a wife's suspected adultery. In what seems to have been an ancient magical rite, the priest announced a curse and wrote it in a book while he made the accused woman drink the water of bitterness. If she were guilty, the curse would take effect in a physical way; if not, she would be set free.

The duty of the priest to effect blessing for the people is most clearly set forth at Numbers 6:22–27 (cf. Deut. 10:8; 21:5). Here in the so-called "Aaronic benediction" which has become part of the Christian heritage, the priests were to pronounce the Lord's blessing upon the people of Israel:

> The Lord bless you and keep you:
> The Lord make his face shine upon you, and be gracious to you:
> The Lord lift up his countenance upon you and give you peace.

The idiom "make the face shine" (*hā'îr pānîm*) is used elsewhere as a synonym for "save" (Ps. 31:16), "restore" (Ps. 80:3, 7, 19; probably also Dan. 9:17), and "redeem" (Ps. 119:134f.). The expression in the following line "lift up the countenance" (*nāsā' pānîm*) elsewhere means "show favor" (Gen. 19:21; 32:20; Deut. 10:17; 28:50; Mal. 1:8, 9; 2:9) or is used adjectively to describe an honored person (Isa. 3:3; 9:15). When the priest pronounced this benediction on behalf of Yahweh, he was actually effecting God's salvation for the congregation. Further, the concluding words from Yahweh to Moses are these: "So shall they put my name upon the people of Israel, and I will bless them" (v. 27). Thus the three-fold blessing became the means by which God was present for the people, for "to put his name there" is used frequently as a deuteronomic formula to express God's presence with the people at the chosen sanctuary (Deut. 12:5, 21; 14:24; 1 Kings 9:3, and often). The benediction then is far more than a routine conclusion to a service of worship.

3. *The Sacrificial System.* Certainly not unrelated to the functions of the priesthood but worthy of special attention is the system for sacrifice, particularly as it is described in an originally independent body at Leviticus 1—7. As is true of virtually every other cultic institution, the sacrifices were phenomena shared by Israel with her Canaanite neighbors. Yet, Israel's sacrifices were interpreted differently: as the gifts of Yahweh, the God who acts in history.

The types of sacrifice in the Old Testament are too numerous to describe here, but a brief summary of the major types might be helpful in determining the significance of the system. (a) The burnt offering (*'ōlâ*) of various animals is described at Leviticus 1:3–17; 6:8–13. As the name implies, the animal was burned in entirety; the smoke ascended (*'ālâ*) to the Lord and was found by him to have a pleasing odor. This sacrifice was a gift to God as a token of gratitude, homage, and reverence. (b) The cereal offering (*minḥâ*) was likewise a gift. According to the instructions at Leviticus 2:1–16; 6:14–18, the offering consisted of flour prepared without leaven. Only a portion of the sacrifice was burned, for the most holy part was eaten by the priests. Both the burnt offering and the cereal offering were gifts to Yahweh. In the Canaanite system gifts were offered to the gods in order to sustain them, that is, to give life and power to the gods who in the course of the seasonal cycle died and needed to be revived. There was a certain magical quality about nature and the cult's effect on the natural process. In the Old Testament this magical notion was rejected in favor of a personal relationship between God and the worshiper.

(c) The peace offering (*zebaḥ*) was eaten, except for the blood in which was the life and for the fat which belonged to the Lord (Lev. 3:1–17; 7:11–36). After separating those two portions, the worshipers and the priests established communion with one another and with Yahweh by participation in a meal. These sacrifices were used for thanksgivings, for vows, and for gifts—all in terms of fellowship with God. (d) The sin offering (*ḥaṭṭā't*) was meant to absolve a priest, a ruler, any individual, or the whole community of an unintentional sin (Lev. 4:1–36; 6:24–30; Num. 15:27–29). The worshiper brought the animal (a bull, goat, or lamb) before the tent of meeting, laid hands on it to transfer the sin, and killed it. The priest sprinkled and poured the blood, burned the fat, and ate the meat, but in the entire process he made atonement for the worshiper, "and he shall be forgiven" (Lev. 4:20, 26, 31). The certainty of this effect is a striking statement of faith and trust in the provisions the Lord made for his people's well-being. (e) The guilt offering (*'āšām*), closely related to the sin offering, is the means by which atonement is made for specific offenses (Lev. 5:1–4; 6:1–5). The instructions, similar to those of the sin offering (5:5–19; 7:1–10), absolve the worshiper of cultic as well as social sins and thus restore him to the "clean" status for participation in the community.

The significance of this sacrificial system must be seen in light of the covenant which the Lord made with Israel. The God who saved his people from bondage and established with them an enduring relationship continued to be present in a personal way in the cult. In order to achieve this fellowship with Israel, Yahweh provided sacrifices as a means of atonement; that is, all the barriers which stand between him and the people must be removed. Thus even sacrifice was actually God's action from the beginning. As von Rad put it, "It was Israel's belief that Jahweh's turning towards her in salvation was not exhausted in historical deeds and in the gracious guidance of individual lives, but that in the sacrificial cult too he had ordained an instrument which opened up to her a continuous relationship with him" (*Old Testament Theology*, I, p. 260).

The instructions for the ark and the tabernacle, the responsibilities of the priests, and the sacrificial system were the means by which the holy God made himself available for fellowship with his people in ancient Israel. The Christian desacralizes places, priests, and days, and the sacrificial system has been brought to an end by God's sacrifice of his own Son on the cross. Thus the instructions in the long section of the Tetrateuch *cannot* be *prescriptive* for the church. Yet in their witness to their own time and place they spoke God's word of promise that he would be present in Israel's midst, and in that witness they are *descriptive* of the way in which Yahweh, the Father of Jesus Christ, reaches out to his people for fellowship and forgiveness.

SELECTED BIBLIOGRAPHY

COMMENTARIES

CASSUTO, UMBERTO. *A Commentary on the Book of Exodus.* Jerusalem: Magnes, 1967.
———. *A Commentary on the Book of Genesis.* 2 vols. Jerusalem: Magnes, 1961, 1964.
CHILDS, BREVARD S. *The Book of Exodus: A Critical Theological Commentary.* The Old Testament Library. Philadelphia: Westminster, 1974.
GUNKEL, HERMANN. *Genesis.* 7th ed. Göttingen: Vandenhoeck & Ruprecht. 1966.
KNIGHT, GEORGE A. F. *Theology as Narration: A Commentary on the Book of Exodus.* Grand Rapids, Mich.: Eerdmans, 1976.
MAYS, JAMES L. *The Book of Leviticus. The Book of Numbers.* The Layman's Bible Commentary. Richmond, Va.: John Knox, 1963.
NOTH, MARTIN. *Exodus: A Commentary.* Translated by J. S. Bowden. The Old Testament Library. Philadelphia: Westminster, 1962.
———. *Leviticus: A Commentary.* Translated by J. E. Anderson. The Old Testament Library. Philadelphia: Westminster, 1965.
———. *Numbers: A Commentary.* Translated by James D. Martin. The Old Testament Library. Philadelphia: Westminster, 1968.
VON RAD, GERHARD. *Deuteronomy: A Commentary.* The Old Testament Library. Philadelphia: Westminster, 1966.
———. *Genesis: A Commentary.* Translated by John H. Marks. The Old Testament Library. Philadelphia: Westminster, 1961. Rev. ed., 1972.
SPEISER, E. A. *Genesis.* The Anchor Bible. Garden City, N. Y.: Doubleday & Co., 1964.
WESTERMANN, CLAUS. *Genesis.* Biblischer Kommentar, Altes Testament. Neukirchen-Vluyn: Neukirchener Verlag, 1974.

STUDIES IN THE TETRATEUCHAL SOURCES AND TRADITIONS

ALT, ALBRECHT. "The God of the Fathers." *Essays on Old Testament History and Religion.* Garden City N.Y.: Doubleday Anchor Books, 1968 (Original copyright 1966).
ANDERSON, BERNHARD W. "The Interpretation of Genesis 1—11." *Journal of Biblical Literature* 97(1978): 23–29.
BEYERLIN, WALTER. *Origins and History of the Oldest Sinaitic Traditions.* Translated by S. Rudman. Oxford: Blackwell, 1965.
BRUEGGEMANN, WALTER. *The Land.* Overtures to Biblical Theology. Philadelphia: Fortress, 1977.
CLEMENTS, RONALD. *Abraham and David: Genesis 15 and Its Meaning for Israelite Tradition.* Studies in Biblical Theology. Second Series, 5. Napierville, Ill.: Alec R. Allenson, 1967.
COATS, GEORGE W. *From Canaan to Egypt: Structural and Theological Context*

for the Joseph Story. The Catholic Biblical Quarterly. Monograph Series, 4. Washington: Catholic Biblical Association of America, 1976.

————. *Rebellion in the Wilderness: The Murmuring Motif in the Wilderness Traditions of the Old Testament.* Nashville: Abingdon, 1968.

CROSS, FRANK M. "The Priestly Work." *Canaanite Myth and Hebrew Epic.* Cambridge, Mass.: Harvard University, 1973.

ELLIS, PETER F. *The Yahwist: The Bible's First Theologian.* Notre Dame, Ind.: Fides Publishers, 1968.

HABEL, NORMAN. *Literary Criticism of the Old Testament.* Guides to Biblical Scholarship. Philadelphia: Fortress, 1971.

JENKS, ALAN W. *The Elohist and North Israelite Traditions.* Society of Biblical Literature Monograph Series, Vol. 22. Missoula, Mont.: Scholars, 1977.

McEVENUE, SEAN E. *The Narrative Style of the Priestly Writer.* Analecta Biblica, 50. Rome: Biblical Institute, 1971.

NICHOLSON, E. W. *Exodus and Sinai in History and Tradition.* Growing Points in Theology. Richmond, Va.: John Knox, 1973.

NOTH, MARTIN. *A History of Pentateuchal Traditions.* Translated by Bernhard W. Anderson. Englewood Cliffs, N.J.: Prentice-Hall, 1972.

VON RAD, GERHARD. "The Form-Critical Problem of the Hexateuch." *Problems in the Hexateuch and Other Essays.* New York: McGraw-Hill, 1966.

RENDTORFF, ROLF. "The 'Yahwist' as Theologian? The Dilemma of Pentateuchal Criticism." *Journal for the Study of the Old Testament* 3(1977): 2–10.

SCHMID, H. H. *Der sogenannte Jahwist.* Beobachtungen und Fragen zur Pentateuchforschung. Zürich: Theologischer Verlag, 1976.

VAN SETERS, JOHN. *Abraham in History and Tradition.* New Haven: Yale University, 1975.

THOMPSON, THOMAS L. *The Historicity of the Pentateuchal Narratives.* Beiheft zur Zeitschrift für alttestamentliche Wissenschaft, 133. New York: W. de Gruyter, 1974.

WESTERMANN, CLAUS. *Creation.* Translated by John J. Scullion, S.J. Philadelphia: Fortress, 1974.

WOLFF, HANS WALTER, and BRUEGGEMANN, WALTER. *The Vitality of Old Testament Traditions.* Atlanta: John Knox, 1975.

OTHER WORKS CITED

BAILEY, LLOYD R. *Where Is Noah's Ark?* Nashville: Abingdon, 1978.

————. "Wood From 'Mount Ararat': Noah's Ark?" *Biblical Archeologist* 40(1977): 137–146.

BRIGHT, JOHN. *Covenant and Promise.* Philadelphia: Westminster, 1976.

CHILDS, BREVARD S. "The Birth of Moses." *Journal of Biblical Literature* 84(1965): 109–122.

COATS, GEORGE W. "An Exposition for the Wilderness Traditions." *Vetus Testamentum* 22(1972): 288–295.

CROSS, FRANK M. "The Divine Warrior in Israel's Early Cult." In *Biblical Motifs,* edited by Alexander Altmann. Cambridge, Mass.: Harvard University, 1966.

————. "Yahweh and the God of the Patriarchs." *Harvard Theological Review* 55(1962): 225–259.

CROSS, FRANK M., and FREEDMAN, DAVID N. "The Song of Miriam." *Journal of Near Eastern Studies* 14(1955): 237–250.

FRANKFORT, HENRI. *Kingship and the Gods: A Study of Ancient Near Eastern Religion as the Integration of Society and Nature.* Chicago: University of Chicago, 1948.

FREEDMAN, DAVID N. "Name of the God of Moses." *Journal of Biblical Literature* 79(1960): 151–156.

FRYMER-KENSKY, TIKVA. "The Atrahasis Epic and Its Significance for Our Understanding of Genesis 1—9." *Biblical Archeologist* 40(1977): 147–155.
GESE, HARTMUT. "The Structure of the Decalogue." *Fourth World Congress of Jewish Studies: Papers*, Vol. 1. Jerusalem, 1967.
HYATT, J. PHILIP. "Was Yahweh Originally a Creator Deity?" *Journal of Biblical Literature* 86(1967): 369–377.
KRAMER, SAMUEL N. "The 'Babel of Tongues': A Sumerian Version." *Journal of the American Oriental Society* 88(1968): 108–111.
LAMBERT, W. G., and MILLARD, A. R. *Atra-ḫasis: The Babylonian Story of the Flood.* Oxford: Clarendon, 1969.
LAUHA, AARRE. *Das Schilfmeermotiv im Alten Testament. Vetus Testamentum,* Supplement, 1963.
MCCURLEY, FOSTER R., JR. " 'And after six days' (Mark 9:2): A Semitic Literary Device." *Journal of Biblical Literature* 93(1974): 67–81.
———. *Proclaiming the Promise.* Philadelphia: Fortress, 1974.
MENDENHALL, GEORGE. *Law and Covenant in Israel and the Ancient Near East.* Pittsburgh: The Biblical Colloquium, 1955.
NICHOLSON, E. W. "The Interpretation of Exodus XXIV 9–11." *Vetus Testamentum* 24(1974): 77–97.
NOTH, MARTIN. *The History of Israel.* 2nd ed. New York: Harper & Row, 1960.
PEDERSEN, JOHANNES. *Israel: Its Life and Culture.* Translated by Aslaug Møller. London: Cumberlege, 1946–1947.
PETTINATO, GIOVANNI. "The Royal Archives of Tell Mardik-Ebla." *Biblical Archeologist* 39(1976): 44–52.
PRITCHARD, JAMES B., ed. *Ancient Near Eastern Texts Relating to the Old Testament.* 3rd ed. Princeton: Princeton University, 1969.
VON RAD, GERHARD. *Der Heilige Krieg im alten Israel.* Göttingen: Vandenhoeck & Ruprecht, 1951.
———. *Old Testament Theology.* 2 vols. Translated by D. M. G. Stalker. New York: Harper & Row, 1962, 1965.
———. "There Remains Still a Rest for the People of God." In *Problems in the Hexateuch and Other Essays.* New York: McGraw-Hill, 1966.
STAMM, JOHANN JAKOB, and ANDREW, MAURICE EDWARD. *The Ten Commandments in Recent Research.* Studies in Biblical Theology, Second Series. Napierville, Ill.: Alec R. Allenson, 1967.
ROBERTSON, DAVID. *The Old Testament and the Literary Critic.* Guides to Biblical Scholarship. Philadelphia, Fortress, 1977.
TUCKER, GENE. "The Legal Background of Genesis 23." *Journal of Biblical Literature* 85(1966): 77–84.
DE VAUX, ROLAND. *The Early History of Israel.* Translated by David Smith. Philadelphia: Westminster, 1978.
ZIMMERLI, WALTHER. *The Old Testament and the World.* Translated by John J. Scullion, S.J. Atlanta: John Knox, 1976.

INDEX OF BIBLICAL PASSAGES

References to pericopes from the Three-Year Lectionary
are in boldface type.